Eleanor Roosevelt

and William DeWitt

362946

UN: TODAY AND TOMORROW

ST. PAUL
PUBLIC LIBRARY

HARPER & BROTHERS, Publishers, New York

UN: TODAY AND TOMORROW

*Copyright, 1953, by Anna Eleanor Roosevelt
and William A. DeWitt*

Printed in the United States of America

All rights in this book are reserved.
No part of the book may be used or reproduced
in any manner whatsoever without written permission except in the case of brief quotations
embodied in critical articles and reviews. For
information address Harper & Brothers
49 East 33rd Street, New York 16, N. Y.

FIRST EDITION

I-C

JX
1977
R78u
COPY 1

Library of Congress catalog card number: 53-8752

Contents

Supplements:

The UN and Human Rights

THE PURPOSE of this book is to tell the day-to-day story of the United Nations in a way that will give it down-to-earth, personal meaning for anyone who reads it. Not the details of parliamentary procedure in the General Assembly, or the delicate subtleties of international law, or all the many-worded names of the hundreds of committees and the long chronology of their meetings, resolutions and reports. But the human story of the UN's work and the people who do it, the methods and objectives, some of the failures and some of the successes.

No one can doubt that the nations which took part in the preliminary conference at Dumbarton Oaks, and later at San Francisco collaborated on the UN charter, were all honestly looking for methods by which they could refashion the world into a design for peaceful living. None of the leaders or the nations they represented were under the delusion that acceptance of the Charter would automatically banish conflict, but they did believe that peace was impossible without observance of its principles. And they hoped under the Charter to construct international machinery that would foster co-operation among nations in the varied fields of human activity and thereby through better mutual understanding increase the desire of all peoples to live without war.

At the first UN meeting in London, during January and February of 1946, this machinery was set up and put in motion. Following the Charter plan, its main parts were the General Assembly, the Security Council, the Economic and Social Council, the Trusteeship

Council, the International Court of Justice and the Secretariat, with subsidiary parts to be added as needed in accordance with the terms of the Charter.

Although the Charter merely says that each member "shall not have more than five representatives in the General Assembly," five alternates in addition were provided for as a continuing rule; however not all members take advantage of this rule. The delegation as a whole casts one vote. A simple, or two-thirds majority, would determine a recommendation, depending on its importance, and no member is entitled to a veto. (The Assembly has no power to do more than recommend courses of action to its members.)

In the vitally important Security Council, however, which is entrusted with the primary responsibility of maintaining peace in the world, five of the eleven members (China, France, the U.S.S.R., the United Kingdom of Great Britain and Northern Ireland, and the United States of America) were given a great advantage. They were designated in the Charter as permanent members and, except on questions of procedure, the required majority of seven for passage of any measure had to include the unanimous affirmatives of all permanent members present and voting. This was the equivalent of veto power for any one of the five nations named. (Abstention, of course, does not constitute a veto.)

In writing this veto power into the Charter the intention had been merely to protect the Great Powers from interference in what they could reasonably define as their domestic affairs by any majority combination of smaller members. But the Soviet member of the Council used it so often and in so many ways other than was originally intended that the General Assembly at last was driven to find methods of getting around the resultant impasses. One method was authorized in a resolution giving the Assembly the right to take up any question no longer under consideration in the Security Council.

Statesmen who had watched the beginning, the fumbling middle and the final failure of the League of Nations felt it essential for the UN to possess an international police force capable of enforcing its decisions. The argument was that individual countries, long accustomed to respect for their familiar internal laws, still needed constabularies to see that obedience continued; how much greater, therefore, the necessity for an adequate security system in this international union, whose regulations were unfamiliar and not invariably acceptable to all countries they affected, and whose members were unused to submitting to any authority higher than themselves. If reason failed to persuade (which must be occasionally expected for a long time till member countries learned to concede the moral authority of international decisions as meekly as Americans had learned to concede the legal authority of the United States Supreme Court), then collective force should be available to bring any recalcitrant into line.

Articles 43-47 of the Charter provided for such a police force in rather general terms. But controversy between the United States and Soviet Russia over control of atomic energy and other aspects of disarmament prevented actual establishment of any UN military organization on a permanent basis. This failure has weakened the UN's prestige and made many of its tasks more difficult than they might have been.

Both pacific and military measures to stop aggression are duties of the Security Council. It shares with the Trusteeship Council obligations to see to the welfare of Trust Territories in the category called "strategic areas." These are wards of UN member nations which regard them as essential to the latters' defense (the Marianas, Marshalls and Caroline Islands are the United States "strategic area" Pacific Trust Territory). Other Trust Territories, without this special classification, come under the single jurisdiction of the Trusteeship Council, which was a particular interest of the government heads who originated the UN idea. The Council has approached the task of administering non-self-governing peoples with a humanitarian regard for their political, economic and cultural interests very different from the old colonial days.

The Economic and Social Council was set up and has operated pretty much as the Charter contemplated, except, possibly, that its work has been expanded and diversified more than was expected, partly in compensation for reverses in other sections of the UN program.

The International Court of Justice is the principal judicial organ of the UN and functions in accordance with a statute embodied in the Charter which was based upon the statute of the Permanent Court of International Justice, the world court it superseded.

The Secretariat, which is housekeeper and administrator for all of the UN, is headed by the Secretary-General and its personnel are selected by him.

The achievements of the many agencies and organizations associated with the Economic and Social Council have been numerous and substantial. Touching as they do on a variety of fascinating areas of life, a number of these achievements will be recounted later in this book.

The Economic and Social Council felt from the beginning that a first essential for any of its work was widespread understanding of the Charter's emphasis on the value of human rights and freedoms and their rightful possession by all people, regardless of race or creed, color or national origin. Recognition of these rights seemed to the Council one of the indispensable cornerstones on which a peaceful world could be built. Therefore, in the spring of 1946, the Council called together a Commission on Human Rights to decide how this could be achieved for all peoples.

Its first job, the Council decided, should be to write a Charter of Human Rights, so that its aims would be clearly set forth and understandable to all the member nations.

Organizing as a group of eighteen members appointed by governments which were selected for being geographically representative, the Commission went to work composing the Charter. But its members decided in the beginning to work at the same time on a declaration which would form the first part of the Charter. This Universal Declaration of Human Rights (see p. 217) was intended to set standards and voice the aspirations of people throughout the world, but not to be legally binding.

Two other parts were planned for the Charter as a whole. One was to be a covenant or covenants written in the form of treaties for ratification by all the nations accepting them, each in accordance with its own constitutional processes. If changes of domestic laws were required to attain the standards of the treaties, they would have to be made.

The third part of the Charter was to be a plan of implementation, its aim being to provide methods of calling to account signatories that failed to live up to their agreements.

Because the Declaration was not legally binding, it was easiest to agree upon, and the final draft was presented through the Economic and Social Council to the General Assembly meeting in Paris in 1948. After nearly two months of discussion the Assembly approved the Declaration, with forty-eight affirmative votes, two nations absent (Honduras and Yemen) and eight abstaining (the Soviets and their satellites, and South Africa and Saudi Arabia).

The reason given by the Communist members for abstention was that the Declaration failed to go beyond the eighteenth century in recognizing rights, that it gave insufficient importance to the new rights of the twentieth century, the economic and social rights, and therefore was valueless.

South Africa, on the other hand, felt that the document went much too far. The delegates said they hoped to give fundamental rights and freedoms to their people, but not such modern ones.

Saudi Arabia abstained because of the article on freedom of conscience and religion, in which it is said that an individual has "the right to change his religion or belief." In an impressive speech before the General Assembly the Foreign Minister from Pakistan, Sir Zafrulla Khan, had justified Moslem adherence to the Declaration, despite this clause, on the ground, as I remember it, that the Koran said he who can believe, shall believe; he who cannot believe, shall disbelieve; the only sin is to be a hypocrite. On the strength of this speech Pakistan, largest of the Moslem states, brought along to the affirmative side all the Arab Moslem states except Yemen, which was absent, and Saudi Arabia. The delegate from Saudi Arabia explained that his King would not accept the interpretation of the Koran put forward by Sir Zafrulla Khan. It did seem a little flexible to other Moslems, but the cause was a good one.

The practical effect of such a Declaration, with no legally binding power, might seem disputable. But, for one thing, the forty-eight accepting states combined their affirmation of the Declaration with a resolution that bound them to acquaint their peoples with its contents so far as they could and to try to attain the standards it set up. For another, new governments arising, such as India and Indonesia, incorporated some of the Declaration's clauses into their constitutions. Here in the United States some courts referred to the document in legal decisions and in one or two cases there was a thought it might carry authority, since it was an extension of the UN Charter, which had been accepted as a treaty by the United States and therefore was the supreme law of the land. This view was not borne out by higher courts.

I think the Declaration's impact on people throughout the world has been of very considerable magnitude—much greater than most Americans suspect. Like the effect of the Magna Carta, the Droit de l'Homme and the Bill of Rights in our own Constitution, it isn't easy to measure, particularly because it's exerted on an international scale, but it's there. As an expression of fundamental UN philosophy it has enormous psychological influence—and some of the psychological influence reverts to the benefit and prestige of the UN.

The UN has translated the Declaration into forty-seven different languages and has set December 10 as Human Rights Day, to be celebrated by all UN member nations.

Work on the covenant part of the Charter has been going on steadily since 1948, but fashioning a feasible treaty form for human rights has proved very difficult. Finally, it was decided to separate the task into two halves—a covenant for civil and political rights and another one for economic and social rights. The first pair are more familiar, more easily phrased in traditional legal phraseology and much of their content is already on the statute books of such countries as our own. Therefore the Commission foresees less trouble gaining their acceptance than if they were combined in one document with economic and social rights, which are much more controversial.

A nondiscrimination clause, though it's part of our Constitution, would rouse antagonism in the United States, but this could be met by inserting the standard federal-state clause which is part of many other American treaties. It binds only the federal government to observe the treaty and only where Federal law is operative, leaving to the states the decision in their jurisdiction. Countries that are not federations of sovereign states, as we are in theory, rather bitterly oppose this clause in our treaties on the ground that it's an evasion of responsibility: they obligate their whole peoples, while we make reservations. Nevertheless, I myself would prefer to risk their displeasure, if adding the clause will make for a step forward, rather than give up all hope of gaining acceptance by our Senate.

One article in the last draft of the civil and political rights covenant that I saw dealt with self-determination of peoples. It failed to explain under what circumstances people should have the right of self-determination. Moreover, in maintaining the right of people to control their own natural resources it made no provision for compensating foreign investors or contractors on the loss of income when such resources are nationalized. Obviously, these omissions alone would prevent United States ratification.

Since the present Administration in Washington announced in advance of their completion that it would not present either of the covenants for ratification to the Senate (nor those on genocide and the political rights of women), there is now less point in speaking about them to Americans, who will not be affected for some time to come, no matter how they are written.

But it might be worth while to consider a question that is sometimes asked: why do we need a treaty? The basic answer is that law is a better framework in which to develop rights and freedoms than waiting for a change in heart by believers in the theory of a master race or the Lord-endowed privilege of one skin color to rule over others. Without a law some who don't need a change in heart hesitate to act on their own beliefs because of social pressures. With a law, they need only obey to do what they consider right.

The third part of the Charter, implementation, presents hard, practical problems. Nongovernmental organizations feel that petitions should be received from sources of their own kind, as well as from individuals. But there is no machinery to handle the great number of complaints sure to come. Already thousands of them are on file in the UN Human Rights Division, waiting for action. Some governments have suggested setting up a Committee on Human Rights composed of members of high standing and many nationalities, from whom panels could be drawn to hear individual cases, with complaints permitted at first only by one state against another. There is a good chance, of course, in such a setup that friendly states would forget to complain against each other, while unfriendly ones would go out of their way to fill the docket. But even this limited and dubious beginning might be better than nothing.

Aside from the adverse attitude of the American Government, there is a good deal of informed and sympathetic opinion in favor of shelving the covenants for the present, while the Declaration is given time to do all the informational ground-breaking it can in preparation for consideration of the actual treaties. My own feeling is that we can't gain ground by standing still.

Human rights and freedoms are essential to the economic development of many areas of the world, as field workers of the Specialized Agencies will attest. Then with health, education and better opportunities to work, new areas can be opened as the additional markets we need for our products. Recognition of human rights and freedoms is thus essential to the preservation of our own standard of living. It's also a vital issue that affects our world leadership among democratic nations.

I hope this book will serve to strengthen the belief of our people in the value of the UN and the absolute necessity of giving it our full support.

ELEANOR ROOSEVELT

UN: TODAY AND TOMORROW

CHAPTER 1

Politics and Shooting

DRIVING to UN Headquarters in the spring of 1953, a passenger admired the beauty of its buildings aloud to her cab driver. He agreed. Then she asked him if he had been inside and he shook his head.

"The guided tours are on seven days a week," she persisted. "You could go on a week end, or whenever you have a day off."

"No. I wouldn't go," he said, without belligerence. "Not that I have anything against them. But I won't go till they stop the war in Korea."

There are a thousand monumental problems facing the UN daily—political, economic, social, technical, administrative questions of the utmost difficulty. But there isn't a harder or more important type of question than the one raised by that cab driver. It recurs again and again in one form or another.

It's easy enough to point out the failure of his logic. But his attitude, which the end of the fighting won't affect, is also the attitude of millions of others, and as an obstacle to understanding it has the rugged height, weight and imperviousness to argument of the Andes Mountain range.

One trouble is that he's right, in a sense. The UN *was* set up to keep peace in the world, and it clearly hasn't. The 140,000 American casualties in Korea are tragic and unanswerable proof of that. And no amount of future international harmony will ever bring back the 25,000 dead.

But the blood and the waste of Korea do not, despite the UN's inability to avoid combat in this case, relieve us of the responsibility and the need for understanding what happened and how, if only as a first step toward preventing future disasters.

The UN *was* set up to keep peace, it's true. But only as a mechanism its members could use if they wished to iron out their differences without resorting to armed force. It has no power to keep nations from starting wars if they so choose. It has no power to stop wars, once started, except by military victory of member forces under its unified command, or by negotiation. What the UN tried in the case of Korea was something unique in the annals of modern warfare—a combination of patient, protracted negotiation and at the same time military action that was powerful enough to stand off the aggressors and demonstrate to them plainly that they could not win, but limited to re-establishment and defense of the South Korean border that existed before the invasion.

Three years of desperate and bloody fighting greatly confused the issues. By June of 1953, when the Communist command agreed to UN truce proposals, only to have South Korean President Syngman Rhee turn on his allies and protectors with "unilateral" actions designed to wreck early peace prospects—by this time most of the background of Korea had been forgotten and in the public mind the name signified only an endlessly drawn-out, lethal and prodigiously costly mess from which we ought to withdraw with what grace we could, but anyhow fast. What we were doing there in the beginning, what the fighting was all about, what anyone hoped to gain, were not only questions that had no clear answers, but questions that weren't even any longer often asked.

Korea as an organized nation antedates the United States by about three thousand years. Without some notion of at least the latter stages of that thirty-century history, it's hard to think of President Rhee's actions during the truce negotiations as anything but irresponsible, if not deranged. But in the light of the inhuman handling of his country as a pawn in the nineteenth-century-and-after designs of Russia, China and, for the thirty-five years before the end of World War II, by Japan, they take on a motivation that's perfectly clear and open to sympathy, even if their intelligence stays equally open to question.

From the twelfth century B.C. on, Korea had close ties with China, culturally and governmentally. Japan made her first major try at invasion in 1592, with an army of 300,000 men. Coming to the rescue with 60,000 men, China fought off the invaders for six years till the death of the Japanese Regent in 1598 called them home. In 1866, 1867 and 1871 United States and French expeditions killed a great many Koreans in retaliation for the deaths of French missionaries and American adventurers at Korean hands, but made no attempt to establish a permanent hold on the peninsula. The second major Japanese conquest effort came in 1894 and this time the Chinese lost out in the fighting. But within a few years Russian intrigue undermined the Japanese position, and it took a smashing victory in the Russo-Japanese War of 1904-1905 (the United States President was mediator for the peace, incidentally) to put the Island Empire firmly in the saddle. Japan formally annexed Korea in 1910.

Anyone looking at the wrecked cities and ravaged countryside today might well ask: "Why? What did they want?"

The answer is: forests of great value in the north; a wealth of mineral deposits waiting to be developed—gold, silver, zinc, copper, lead, iron, tungsten, graphite, kaolin and hard coal; and a highly important strategic location. It was this last that the Japanese said forced them into the 1904 conflict with Russia. Japan called the peninsula a "dagger pointed at her heart."

Japanese rule over Korea was barbarously repressive, with torture and execution the answer to protest, and planted the seeds of an independence movement that grew steadily and passionately through the years till the final Allied victory in the Pacific in 1945 made the generation-long dream of release come true.

"Half-true" would be more accurate. Soviet forces occupied the northern portion of the peninsula at the end of the war, while the United States Army occupied the southern part, below the 38th Parallel. A provisional government composed of five representatives each from the two areas, together with the Joint Commission of the

Occupying Powers, was supposed to work out a plan for independence after a four-power trusteeship (the United States, Soviet Russia, the United Kingdom and China) lasting five years. But the Joint Commission never came close to agreeing on anything, the two halves of the land remained divided and in the latter part of 1947 the United States submitted the problem to the UN.

Moscow promptly objected that, like other questions connected with the peace treaties, this was out of the UN's jurisdiction. But the General Assembly went ahead and set up a Temporary Commission on Korea whose job it was to arrange free elections for a national assembly, which, in turn, would set up a national government. The Soviet bloc at the UN refused to have any part of this action, on the ground that absence of elected Korean representatives made it a violation of the UN Charter, and guards along the 38th Parallel prevented the Commission from going north of there to do its work.

Nevertheless, the election was announced for May 10, 1948, with UN field groups observing, and, although the Soviet Government in the north hastily, on May 1, adopted a constitution claiming jurisdiction over all Korea, it went off on schedule and was declared by the UN observers to be a free and valid expression of will by the two-thirds of the Korean population living south of the 38th Parallel. The Government of the Republic of Korea came into being, with Syngman Rhee as President, and on December 12, 1948, the UN General Assembly gave it official blessing, asking that the occupying powers withdraw their forces and setting up a new Commission on Korea to lend good offices toward unification of the whole peninsula.

In 1949 this Commission reported to the General Assembly that it had observed the withdrawal of United States forces in accordance with the UN request, but had been "unable to verify" the withdrawal of Soviet occupation troops for the good reason that it had been denied permission to cross the 38th Parallel. It confessed total failure in unification efforts, for the same reason, and mentioned bitter propaganda and hostile activities on both sides. In early 1950 the Commission learned of incidents along the border and of guerrilla activity within the Republic to the south. As a result, it appointed military observers and they were in position, on June 25, to report expeditiously when the full-scale invasion began.

The United States that same day announced our opinion of the invasion as a breach of the peace and an act of aggression, requesting an immediate meeting of the UN Security Council. For once the Soviet veto failed to stop action, the Russian permanent member being absent, and under United States urging the Security Council in a quick series of meetings undertook to resist the attack with UN member forces under a unified command headed by the United States, which was also to appoint the commander. President Truman designated General Douglas A. MacArthur to lead the UN forces, and the fight was on.

All the rest is well remembered—the retreats and advances of the troops, with their concomitant misery and heroism, losses and victories; the overt addition of Chinese Communist armies to the aggressors; the political uproar in the United States when General MacArthur was relieved and took his case before Congress with the dramatic "old soldier" speech; the arguments of later returning generals over the question whether or not there was enough ammunition and whether or not we should have mounted an all-out offensive; the sudden hope in mid-1951 when the Russians themselves suggested discussing a cease-fire, and the dwindling of it after actual talks began and got nowhere; the rekindling in mid-1953 when the Communists at last stopped stalling and accepted the UN truce proposals formulated by the Indians, and the eleventh-hour dashing of that by the South Koreans' unauthorized release of prisoners of war; then the beginning of recovery from shock as the Communists took it with less umbrage than we had expected; and, finally, the cease-fire itself.

Clearly, Korea has been a hard test for the UN, both as a concept for furthering world peace and as a mechanism for implementing the concept. There were tests before, but they rarely got to open fighting—never on the scale of Korea—and they were both briefer and less complex in their possible consequences. This was the sternest of trials for will power, patience, endurance, the spirit of co-operation and the willingness to negotiate and compromise. There is a great deal to be learned from it now, and there will be more as time goes on, for the issues over which the fighting began were not settled either by firing the cannon or by ceasing to fire the cannon. They remain where they were, no matter what that taxi driver does about the guided tours.

For fire-eaters one of the most painful lessons to be memorized is adapting ourselves, as Secretary-General Hammarskjold puts it, to war "which ends without total victory for any party but only for a principle." Americans tend to pride themselves on the somewhat debatable point that we've emerged victorious from all conflicts except Korea; hence the recurrent demand from some quarters during the fighting that we plunge forward, no matter what the cost, to the Yalu River and, if resistance by the enemy continued, go on to bring the whole of continental China to its knees.

The victory for a principle (the principle, of course, being unified international protection against aggression), Mr. Hammarskjold said, "is a full vindication of those brave men who have sacrificed their lives. . . ." This is a novel attitude that the parents, loved ones and friends of the dead may find it difficult to accept. Traditionally, there have been heroes in both victories and lost causes. That there may be heroes in a deliberate stalemate is a new idea, acclimatization to which undoubtedly will require time.

Finally, Mr. Hammarskjold insisted, the victory for a principle "will have to be followed by a peace without vengeance. The United Nations Charter provides for all manners of action to repel aggression but it makes no provision for the ultimate punishment of the aggressor, once the fruits of an attempted aggression have been taken from him. The United Nations . . . does not foresee the use of force to secure the fruits of victory in terms of land and power."

This, again, breaks with ancient, punitive tradition that demanded an eye for an eye, with perhaps a nose thrown in for good measure. The tradition is immensely strong, but if it seems infrangible we can recall powerful other traditions that have yielded to the pressure of reality in our times. "They started it, didn't they?" may well go the way of Calvin Coolidge's celebrated "They hired the money, didn't they?" If we were able to accept the fact of life that it's sometimes impossible and even undesirable to force repayment of dollars loaned, we have a chance of learning that it's impossible to obtain restitution for lives and treasure lost in a "victory for principle" and in the long run bad judgment to try.

Another painful truth we are learning is that it's not only the aggressor we need to watch, but also the weaker nation we're trying to protect. An underdog, to survive, gets the habit of snatching at any and every advantage, without much more regard to the effect on friend than on foe. When Syngman Rhee released the prisoners of war, he admitted his purpose was to forestall a truce and keep the UN forces fighting till the Communists were driven out of Northern Korea and the whole peninsula was united under his Government. In effect, he accused the UN of breaking faith by not pursuing that military objective on its own.

The truth, of course, is that the plainly stated military objective of the UN, as translated into action chiefly by United States arms, equipment and manpower, was to re-establish and protect the pre-aggression border on the 38th Parallel. Unification of the two divided sections of Korea was stated with equal plainness to be a political objective, still aimed at, but which the UN proposed to achieve only by peaceful means.

Of UN intervention to the end of June, 1953, Korean Ambassador You Chan Yang said it had done nothing for the Republic, except, he inferred, bring on destruction. "We are still in terrible fear that the Communists will occupy our country sooner or later." So, the UN might answer, are other countries, and: "We've done everything we thought we could in Korea, but there is a larger question we have to keep in mind: the danger of a third world war. What you want us to do now might well bring it on." As for the destruction, the UN Unification and Rehabilitation Commission is still on the ground, waiting to do its part in repairing damage.

The Korean conflict brought practical changes in the working of the UN, as well as new ideas about warfare for public consumption. Chief among these was a shift of functional emphasis from the Security Council to the General Assembly.

When the Charter was signed in San Francisco, June 26, 1945, a fundamental premise of the UN structure assumed that the five Great Powers allied in World War II would continue to agree on major questions at least. Therefore, although the main body, the General Assembly, gave one equal vote to each of the member nations and required at most a two-thirds majority of those present and voting for action on "important questions," the Security Council got the veto. Composed of eleven members, six of them elected by the Assembly for two-year terms, the Security Council had the primary responsibility for maintaining international peace. Since the Great Powers (China, France, the U.S.S.R., the United Kingdom and the United States) after World War II would be the source of the world's main military strength and had by far the biggest stake in keeping the peace, they were made permanent members of the Council and it was agreed that the Council could take no action against which any one of them voted. The aim of this decision, of course, was to prevent any combination of smaller countries from forcing irresponsible action, the burden and consequences of which would fall most heavily upon the Great Powers.

Unfortunately, the premise turned out to be false. After the war's end, Soviet Russia, instead of going along with the other four Great Powers on matters of importance, almost invariably opposed them, and its own ideas were about equally resisted by the rest. The Security Council became a study in futility and frustration, with East and West at irreconcilable odds on practically everything from disarmament to the old, old problem of Trieste. It was only the accident of Russia's temporary absence from the Council that permitted such prompt UN resistance in Korea.

On the return of the Soviet member August 1, the now familiar veto deadlock again made its appearance. Soviet resolutions accusing the United States of bombing defenseless civilians were rejected eight to one. A United States resolution condemning the North Koreans fell under the Russian single-vote veto. But, since the veto counted only in substantive matters and procedural questions could be decided by a majority of seven Council members, it was possible to forward some of the points being debated to the General Assembly, where the two-thirds majority rule applied and no single nation or small bloc of nations could hamstring positive action.

The intervention of Chinese Communist forces was one of these points. A cease-fire group of the Assembly sent proposals to the People's Republic of China suggesting steps toward a truce, which would be followed by a conference to settle Far Eastern problems, including the question of Formosa and representation of Communist China in the UN. In replying, the Chinese demanded as a basis of agreement the withdrawal of all foreign troops from Korea and leaving the settlement of Korean domestic affairs to the Korean people themselves. They insisted that the "rightful place" of the People's Republic of China in the UN be established as from the beginning of the conference, and that the subject matter of the negotiations must include withdrawal of United States armed forces from Formosa. The idea, of course, was to minimize the Chinese share in the Korean invasion by pinning the label of aggressor in Formosa on the United States, and also to emphasize its claim of being discriminated against by denial of representation in the UN, while the vestigial Chinese Nationalist Government, confined to authority only over the island of Formosa, retained its seat and its veto as a Great Power in the Security Council. To the Chinese and Russian Communists, Formosa was an integral part of China and American interference an act of aggression.

Generally speaking, of course, the United States position was upheld in the Assembly and additional measures, including embargoes, were taken against the aggressors.

As early as September, 1950, weaknesses of Security Council organization in an emergency had become so apparent that the United States submitted to the General Assembly a "United Action for Peace" plan, which formalized the shift in emphasis from the

Security Council to the Assembly in case of threats to peace or acts of aggression. Its chief provision was for emergency special sessions of the Assembly on twenty-four hours' notice at the request of seven members of the Security Council or a majority of UN member states, if the Security Council, through disagreement among its permanent members, failed to act in a threat to or breach of peace. The minority objected that the United States plan, by depriving the Security Council of a portion of its powers, in effect changed the Charter, and it also resisted convening the Assembly on only twenty-four hours' notice and by the vote of only seven Security Council members. But on November 3, 1950, the American proposals won, fifty-two to five, and the UN's ability to act in a crisis was thereby considerably increased.

Ultimate settlement of Korea's problems probably must await a general political settlement in the Far East, or at the minimum, establishment of some workable *modus vivendi*, which may or may not come out of the conferences to follow the truce. What can be said now of the UN's part in the affair is nothing very new. The fledgling organization, still learning the ABC's of a One World culture, met its greatest crisis without falling apart—which is not nearly so negative as it may sound. In so doing it provided history's first dramatic example of a permanently organized international body resisting aggression with military force, and resisting it successfully. It not only stood off a powerful initial attack and won back ground yielded in the beginning, but maintained its purpose and its principles undiminished through long months and years of painful military attrition and exasperating shifts, procrastination and provocation in the negotiations for a truce. And it became internally stronger during the trial.

These items surely belong on the credit side of the ledger and offer hope for greater accomplishments in the future as the eight-year-old organization grows up and becomes wiser and more articulate—more able, for one thing, to persuade citizens of its member countries that it's their role to help make it succeed, not to sit back and demand miracles in a vacuum. Our taxi driver friend is one example.

There were crises before Korea. Professors Amry Vandenbosch and Willard N. Hogan have made interesting brief studies of the seventeen disputes or dangerous situations that were referred to the Security Council, the General Assembly, or both, up to September of 1951, judging what success or lack of it the UN had in dealing with each case. In their opinion the UN had had half a dozen reasonably well-defined successes, four problems in which it made some progress or improvement occurred for other reasons, and seven in which it failed or could not act.

This is a somewhat arbitrary accounting, with which the professors might not altogether agree. For instance, in January of 1946 the Government of Iran asked to have alleged interference by the Soviet Union in its internal affairs brought before the Security Council. The Security Council referred the question back to Iran and Russia for further negotiation, asking to be kept informed. In March Iran again complained, stating that Soviet troops being maintained in Iranian territory contrary to treaty provisions were a danger to international peace and security. The Security Council discussed the matter and decided to delay action a few weeks, but keep the complaint on its agenda. Soviet troops then withdrew and further discussion was adjourned. Despite a lack of formal action by the Security Council, this case has a flavor of accomplishment and goes down in the count as a success.

On the other hand, the case of Franco Spain is placed in the zero column. At the San Francisco and Potsdam conferences it had been decided to deny membership in the UN to the Spanish dictatorship, which had given aid and comfort to Hitler and Mussolini. In early 1946 this decision was endorsed by the General Assembly. A month or two later Poland charged in the Security Council that Franco's activities had caused international friction and were a danger to international peace and security. Russia wanted to take concrete measures to overthrow the Spanish regime, but the others wouldn't go that far. In December the General Assembly barred Spain from membership in international agencies and conferences connected with the UN (a ban that was lifted in 1950), asked member countries to recall their ambassadors from Madrid and instructed the Security Council to think of a course of action if Spain failed to establish a new and acceptable government. All this might be called action, but Franco remains in command of Spain (receiving financial aid, as a matter of fact, from the United States), and therefore the aim of the original discussion has not been achieved and the case goes down as a failure so far as effective UN action is concerned, whatever we may think of the wisdom of the Assembly's recommendations.

In the Corfu Channel affair, brought before the Security Council in January of 1947 by the British, Albania was accused of laying a minefield without notification that damaged two British warships and killed British sailors. Albania sat in on the Security Council meeting and heard the British resolution against her lose by virtue of a Soviet veto. But the Council, on a procedural vote not affected by the veto, then recommended that both parties submit the case to the Court of International Justice. Great Britain followed this advice and, despite Albanian protests over the Court's jurisdiction, eventually won a judgment of £843,947. This instance falls into the middle group of accounting, in which problems are resolved or changed for reasons other than Assembly or Security Council action.

In February of 1946 the governments of Syria and Lebanon made a complaint to the Security Council that was almost identical with the one presented by Iran the month before, only this time it was French and British troops, rather than Russian, that were alleged to be trespassing. The result was the same, too, the troops being withdrawn without any formal request or direction from the Council. Accomplishment.

A clearer-cut success for the Security Council was Indonesia, one of the earliest and not one of the easiest problems it had to face. The Ukrainian S.S.R. submitted it first on January 12, 1946, charging that British and Japanese military actions against Indonesians threatened international peace and security. Nothing happened then, but the following year, after the Netherlands had agreed, in March, to independence for the Republic of Indonesia, Australia and India called the Council's attention to fighting between the Dutch and the Indonesians. A Council Good Offices Committee went to Java in October and arranged a truce, which was signed January 17, 1948. But trouble started again and continued all through 1948, the Netherlands in December denouncing the truce agreement and starting military operations in earnest. On January 28, 1949, the Security Council called on both sides to stop shooting and on the Netherlands to release the Indonesian President and other political figures being held prisoner. At UN instigation Dutch and Indonesian representatives then held meetings from April to August and, with the help of the UN Commission for Indonesia (the Good Offices Committee with expanded authority), agreed on most of the disputed points. That November at The Hague a complete transfer of sovereignty over Indonesia was promised to the Republic of the United States of Indonesia by December 30 and the Netherlands-Indonesian Union was established, a co-operative federation of equal members to handle foreign affairs and defense, and financial, economic and cultural matters. On September 28, 1950, the General Assembly took in the Republic of Indonesia as the sixtieth member of the UN.

The celebrated Berlin blockade, with its fourteen-months-long air-ferrying of coal, food and other domestic necessities into the German capital, was brought before the Security Council by France, the United States and the United Kingdom on September 29, 1948, but the Soviet veto prevented action and it wasn't until the end of May, 1949 (the blockade started April 1, 1948), that direct agreement reached by representatives of the four occupying powers restored transportation to a common sense level. This was, of course, a failure for the Security Council.

The Communist *coup d'état* of February 25, 1948, in Czechoslovakia came before the Council in March of that year by way of a Chilean request to consider a plea from Dr. Jan Papanek, up till the overthrow of President Beneš the permanent representative of Czechoslovakia to the UN, for an investigation of the change in the Czechoslovakian Government. Russia naturally denounced the allegations of Soviet interference and threats to use force as completely false and intended to divide the Great Powers and weaken the UN. Newly Communist Czechoslovakia declined a Council invitation to talk the matter over on the ground that the Charter did not cover discussion of a country's internal affairs. The Soviet veto expectably blocked further action and the Council remained, in the apt technical phrase, "seized of the question." Total failure.

After Cardinal Mindszenty, Roman Catholic Primate of Hungary, had been sentenced on February 8, 1949, to life imprisonment for treason, the General Assembly adopted a resolution (April 30, 1949) expressing grave concern over the accusations leveled against Hungary and Bulgaria and drawing their attention to clauses in the peace treaties they had signed ensuring respect for human rights and fundamental freedoms. Later, after a carefully considered but practically unhelpful decision by the International Court of Justice against Bulgaria, Hungary and also Rumania (which was brought into the dispute after the first two countries), the Assembly passed a resolution condemning the three nations, none of which was or is a member of the UN. Cardinal Mindszenty, more than four years later, was still confined. In this case, action but no practical achievement.

In Greece, the UN helped to restore a measure of order after trouble with guerrillas supplied by hostile neighboring countries. In a dispute between India and South Africa over alleged discriminatory treatment of Indians in the latter country, no progress was made. And so it goes.

For many of the questions brought before the Assembly and the Council it's necessary to send groups of observers or negotiators, or a combination of both, to the scene of trouble. For these "Investigations and Inquiries" the UN Field Service provides administration and a variety of other services. Mission and Field Service members often lead adventurous lives, full of emergencies and troubles and need for local adaptation. They get "jungle-happy" on long stints in the wilds, they get neuroses from the continual hostility of natives in some of the places they stay, they get shot at, and sometimes they get killed.

Palestine, a relative success among the Security Council and Assembly efforts to resolve international quandaries, has been one of their most complex and difficult problems, with every explosive element of modern life—political, economic, religious, cultural and environmental—dramatically represented and violently conflicting with parallel elements in neighboring countries. The field work of UN observers reflected the situation. It was here that assassins machine-gunned UN Mediator Count Folke Bernadotte to death and won him the legend of being the first man on earth to lose his life violently in the cause of internationally espoused labor for peace.

(To keep the record straight, this doubtful honor really belongs to Thomas Wasson, United States Consul in Jerusalem and member of the Security Council Truce Commission, who was killed four months earlier, on May 22, 1948, by snipers' bullets. And four other UN representatives similarly preceded Bernadotte to the grave— the Frenchman Labarrière by hand grenade, the Norwegian Ole Bakke by sniper and the Frenchmen Jeannel and Queru shot by a mob as they landed a scout plane.)

The background of the Palestine problem is well enough known: the long desire of the Jewish people for a homeland, the World War I White Paper in which the British held out hope for its realization, the British Mandate after that war which never could work out a solution, the resistance of Arabs who lived in the territory and countries surrounding it, the conflicting religious and ownership claims to the Holy City of Jerusalem, the proclamation of the new State of Israel after termination of the Mandate (May 15, 1948), and the ensuing confused hostilities between Arabs and Israelis.

Before the British Mandate ended, the General Assembly tried its hand at formulating a plan, finally deciding on a scheme of partition into Arab and Jewish States combined in an economic union to be called Palestine, with controversial Jerusalem as a separate unit under the UN trusteeship system. This plan won equal and enthusiastic disapproval from both sides. The Jews ignored it and set up their own State of Israel which the United States and other countries recognized, whereupon the Arabs came in with their rifles. UN efforts had to be redirected toward halting the bloodshed.

On June 11 the Security Council succeeded in achieving a four-week truce and Belgium, France and the United States as members of the UN Truce Commission sent military observers, along with fifty volunteers mostly from the security guard at Lake Success, to keep watch on both sides. The story of this Field Service operation may not be typical of all the others, particularly since it was early in the UN's experience of such things, but it has points of interest.

A Field Service administrator (actually, there was no Field Service then; he was a staff member of the division of the Secretariat's Conference and General Services Department that later became Field Service) arrived in Cairo June 12, the day after the truce began, to take care of the twenty-one military observers originally scheduled to be supplied by France, Belgium and the United States. His first problem was to find field equipment, such as tents and stoves, and transportation. He was lucky to get his hands on four C-47 transports, not only because they could move his charges, but also because the plane crews bore out transport pilots' wide reputation as able scroungers: they uncovered any number of necessary items that were hidden from ordinary view. But for ground transport in the beginning he had to depend on the jeeps and trucks of the belligerents, and the military observers sometimes got the idea that they were seeing only what the side whose vehicles they were riding in wanted them to see. If the radio equipment available had seen better days, it was long before, and the mission rarely knew when its messages were getting through to Mediator Bernadotte, who was on the island of Rhodes.

The mission moved to Haifa on June 25, to be closer to the area of operations. Radio communication improved then and the British

Middle East Office demonstrated Anglo-UN solidarity by lavishly raiding its own supplies, to the consternation of the accounting department, which took three years to straighten out the debits and credits, probably never discovering where to charge some of the items.

Among members of the mission the consensus was that both sides observed this first truce with reasonable scrupulousness. Partly, the absence of shooting stemmed from activities of the observers themselves. A Secretariat member named John Reedman, for instance, once learned of Arab and Israeli groups approaching each other with maleficent intentions. He promptly grabbed a jeep and a large white flag and patrolled a highway between the two groups, driving the jeep with one hand back and forth, with the other waving the flag—also shouting "Stop." Oddly enough, it worked. Both would-be combatant groups quieted down and went away without firing a shot.

Other observers tried the same stunt, with varying success, during the first truce, but a few educational bullet wounds taught them all caution in later times.

One cause of trouble was that Arab farmers around Haifa who had planted crops in the early spring insisted on returning to harvest them. The Israelis understandably took potshots at them. And observers in the Haifa area had another extraordinary local situation. There was a forest through the center of which ran the imaginary Arab-Israel boundary line. Three or four times between early June and the end of the truce in July patriotic arsonists set it afire. When fire-fighters appeared bullets went pinging through the flames—and military observers ducked without dignity behind any handy tree.

The truce expired on July 9 and the Arabs refused to renew it. Fighting broke out again and in the absence of directions from the Security Council the observers made a kind of tactical retreat to Beirut. The administrator retired to Rhodes to devise new plans for the future. Information began to trickle in to him, its main theme being that he would have three hundred rather than a couple of dozen military observers under his wing. Eventually they reached a count of six hundred.

To get independent mobility for this larger corps of observers, 150 British jeeps were purchased, but Israel refused entry to the British ship chartered to bring them in, and a motley crew of steersmen, including full Army colonels and any number of Navy commanders, were impressed to drive them across the desert. A similar oversight occurred with aircraft, which were chartered from the British, with British pilots to fly them. These, too, were barred from Israel, and pilots of other nationalities had to be found and the planes' registry changed before they could be used.

Meanwhile, though fighting with the Arabs continued and new hostilities broke out with the Egyptians in the Negev that fall, the administrative problems of the mission eased down, with larger office space and more experienced help, to the point where buying mechanical parts for the 150 jeeps constituted one of the most serious worries.

Any number of resolutions, representations and suggestions were made by the Security Council and the Assembly. Disturbances flared and subsided, flared and subsided again, till at last, between February and July, 1949, a series of armistices were signed by Israel with Egypt, Lebanon, Jordan and Syria. On May 11, 1949, Israel was accepted as a member of the UN, and it would be pleasant to cite the date as a happy ending. Unfortunately, the Truce Supervision Organization and the Conciliation Commission were still mentioned in the Field Service budget for 1953, and guards along the Israel borders still get their pictures in the papers, with nervous fingers on their triggers.

Reception for UN missions depends on the country. In Korea there has been a warm welcome, in India toleration, in Palestine reluctant toleration, in Somaliland and Eritrea (where the chief business is settling land disputes going back to Mussolini) graceful acceptance by the Italians, in the Balkans welcome by the Greeks and the reverse by the rest. The official list of UN missions personnel dead is twenty-three—thirteen accidents, one suicide, one death by natural causes and eight killed. Members that escape accident, sickness and injury usually at least suffer from the strain of their work and surroundings—their weight falls off, their tempers disintegrate and their general efficiency goes below par. Hence, even those who volunteer to stay on rarely are kept more than a year on one tour of duty.

Aside from its primary concern with peace and international security, the General Assembly, as the "centerpiece" of the UN organization, may consider and act on anything and everything within the scope of UN powers, including visas for Soviet wives of foreign nationals. One vital question, which troubled the writers of the Charter, still troubles the Assembly and everyone else with a stake in the UN, and probably will continue to be bothersome for a long time to come, is the question of voting.

The so-called veto, which is a negative vote by a permanent member of the Security Council that blocks any decision other than those on matters of procedure, has been the subject of much discussion and hard thinking ever since the UN was born. As far back as 1946, the Assembly requested the permanent members to do everything they could to avoid having their special voting privilege impede the Council in reaching prompt decisions. The next year the Assembly put the problem up to its Interim Committee (the so-called "Little Assembly" that sat when the General Assembly was not in session) for other suggestions. As a result of the Interim Committee's studies the Assembly in 1949 passed a resolution defining thirty-five kinds of Council decisions as procedural and therefore not subject to the veto. In addition, the Assembly asked the permanent members to determine among themselves the types of decisions on which they would be willing to withhold a decisive negative vote after seven affirmatives already had been cast. Finally, it asked for consultation among the permanent members before important decisions so as to assure unanimity whenever possible, and perhaps now and then gain an abstention if the opposing member considered the matter of not too vital importance. The point here, of course, is that,

while the Charter requires for any Council decision unanimity of
the permanent members present and voting, it does not require all
of them either to be present or to vote. If the opposing member is
absent or abstains, the measure may pass.

The voting problem includes the highly debatable question of
government representation. China under General Chiang Kai-shek
had the status of a Great Power and was so admitted to the UN as
a charter member, with one of the five veto votes in the Council.
But Chiang no longer has any authority over continental China,
only over his Formosan refuge, and the Communist regime at
Peiping repeatedly demands to be given the "rightful place" Chiang's
representatives still hold in the Assembly and the Security Council.
There are a number of legal points involved, on the basis of which
Secretary-General Trygvie Lie, on March 8, 1950, wrote a memo-
randum to the Security Council stating his opinion that, if the new
government were shown by inquiry to exercise effective internal
authority and to be habitually obeyed by the bulk of the Chinese
population, it would be appropriate for the UN to grant it the right
of representation. In 1951, however, a proposal to consider the question in the Council was rejected on a five-to-five vote (seven affirmative votes only were needed, since this was a procedural matter),
with the United Kingdom on this occasion casting its ballot on the
Soviet side.

The adversaries of Communism are understandably cool to the
idea of adding another presumptive veto to their troubles, but their
moral position isn't altogether comfortable, since the Peiping regime
gives no external evidence of lacking internal authority and the
suicidal mass attacks in Korea signified anything but a failure of
obedience. One compromise suggestion put forth is that the permanent membership of China in the Security Council be abolished,
while delegates from both Peiping and Formosa are seated with
ordinary voting rights in the General Assembly.

Interest in the veto and Chinese representation has tended to
minimize public contemplation of other aspects of the voting question that could in the long run turn out to be far more important.

Besides the other reasons the Charter writers had in mind for providing the veto power, there was the aim of compensating for
disparities in General Assembly voting arrangements. It has been
calculated that a thirty-one-vote majority in the Assembly could be
counted from nations representing only 5.5 per cent of the total
population of the UN's sixty members. The two-thirds majority
needed for major decisions could be had by votes representing only
11 per cent of the total population. Moreover, the twenty-one
smallest member nations, with 2.3 per cent of the population, could
stop any measure that required a two-thirds majority.

In the face of the theatrical conflict between Communist-con-
trolled countries and much of the rest of the world we tend to lose
sight of other considerations, such as the fact made evident during
the Korean conflict that a number of great nations which normally
have gone along with our point of view in opposing Russia may
sometimes entertain reservations and certainly are more open-
minded about the Kremlin than we once deluded ourselves into
believing. In Asia there appeared a political outlook that wasn't,
perhaps, equidistant between Washington and Moscow, but certainly responded to visual stimuli occurring well eastward of the
Potomac. Clearly, the world isn't yet reduced to a two-power system.

In our own hemisphere there is the possibility of a General
Assembly veto not intended by the Charter writers and little considered by U.S. citizens occupied with worrying over the Communists. It's an arithmetical fact that the Latin-American countries
in the UN, acting together, come within a single vote of being able
to block any important measure. They have twenty votes among
them now; all they need for an effective veto is to pick up one extra
from among the other forty nations. As an immediate cause for worry
this Latin-American potentiality has little to recommend it, since the
countries to our south are well equipped with differences among
themselves and so far have not been ostentatiously eager to upset
any major plans of ours. But it's there, nonetheless.

Voting procedures in the Assembly and Security Council are admittedly a paramount weakness of the UN. Many remedies have

been suggested, but none that would suit all interested parties and none that seems attractive enough to win the necessary votes for a change of the Charter.

In the other two main branches of the UN under the General Assembly, the Trusteeship Council and the Economic and Social Council, voting is not the issue that it is in either the Security Council or the Assembly itself, since decisions are reached by a simple majority of the members present and voting.

The Trusteeship Council is one of the UN's two chief methods of watching over and helping the hundreds of millions of people in the world who do not own governments of their own. It is a revised and improved version of the old League of Nations system of mandates, with many obligations for Administering Authorities to help the peoples under their control, economically, educationally and in the development of self-government and other free institutions.

To become a Trust Territory an area must have the country responsible for it present the draft of a Trust Agreement for approval by the General Assembly. The agreements vary, but most contain these basic elements: a definition of the territory, name of the proposed Administering Authority, a description of its rights and obligations, and its promise to submit any dispute with another UN member over interpretation or application of the agreement to the International Court of Justice.

Trust Territories classified as "strategic areas" fall under the primary jurisdiction of the Security Council, but the Trusteeship Council attends to most of their needs not connected with the security of their Administering Authorities or other aspects of international peace.

Administering Authorities are required annually to report on the Trust Territories to the Trusteeship Council. The standard questionnaire prepared by the Council contains 247 detailed queries, and its members or suborgans dig still more deeply into special situations.

Natives of the Trust Territories, or any other individuals or organizations for that matter, have the right to comment or complain to the Trusteeship Council, and close to a thousand of these petitions have received its consideration.

Every three years, approximately, each Trust Territory is visited by a mission from the Council to provide a firsthand view of the situation and permit questioning on subjects that might have escaped the reports.

With information so gathered the Trusteeship Council argues over the quality of administration in the Territories, of which there are a dozen, with six Administering Authorities (some countries administer more than one Territory), and argues further over recommendations for improvement. When the arguments are resolved, the recommendations are sent to the General Assembly and, if approved, are given in its name to the Administering Authorities. One recommendation of the Assembly that especially pleased the Trusteeship Council was that the UN flag should be flown alongside the flags of the Administering Authorities in all Trust Territories.

Non-Self-Governing Territories that do not belong to the Trusteeship System include more than three score areas such as Hawaii, Jamaica, Alaska, Bermuda, French West Africa, Tunisia, Barbados, the Belgian Congo, Hong Kong, Singapore and many others. The countries administering them report annually, not to the Trusteeship Council, but to the Secretary-General. Most have had charge of the Territories for a long time and the main change that came with the UN relationship was assumption of a definite obligation to place the interests of the Territories' inhabitants ahead of everything else.

This concern with the rights of all people to human freedom, economic advancement and eventual self-government is the chief trend since World War II in the development of governmentally dependent areas. Acquisition of colonies for home gain is no longer the form of big-nation rivalry it once was, and, while human enslavement goes on in one way or another, the years since the UN's beginning have seen the freeing from foreign rule of no less than 800,000,-000 men, women and children. This is a figure worth remembering when less fortunate things happen.

Partly because events beyond control have reduced its purely political effectiveness and weakened its direct power to maintain peace among all nations, the UN has turned perhaps more than was originally intended toward helping the world economically, socially and culturally. The third of its main councils, the Economic and Social, is primarily responsible for these phases of its work.

ECOSOC, as it plainly had to be nicknamed, owns an almost interminable list of responsibilities, too varied for quick and easy classification. Just to start with, it found economic questions more answerable on a regional basis and therefore set up three Economic Commissions to deal with them, in Europe, in Asia and the Far East, and in Latin America. Then it broke its job down further into functional commissions and subcommissions such as the Commission on Human Rights, the ones on Narcotic Drugs and Transport and Communications, the Fiscal Commission, the Statistical Commission, Social Commission, Commission on the Status of Women and the Population Commission.

Standing committees deal with Technical Assistance, Negotiations with Specialized Agencies, Non-Governmental Organizations, the Agenda and the interim consideration of the Program of Meetings, which must be a traffic problem.

Among a group of "special bodies" attached to ECOSOC is the UN International Children's Fund (UNICEF). And there is, of course, a variety of *ad hoc* committees to do any odd jobs that come along.

In the economic field ECOSOC is most directly concerned with the improvement of international trade, with statistical development all over the world (many figures on national incomes, for instance, are far short of accurate), with conservation of resources and with transport and communications, but it also has a busy hand in the various programs of Technical Assistance for underdeveloped countries. It works through one standing committee with eight of the Specialized Agencies, such as the Food and Agriculture Organization, World Health Organization and UNESCO, on their individual and co-ordinated plans, and through another with the Technical

Assistance Administration itself, which, along with helping the Specialized Agencies, has its own favorite programs, including the UN advisory social welfare services and training in public administration.

In the social, humanitarian and cultural fields ECOSOC deals with human rights, freedom of information, trade union rights, forced labor, slavery, protection of minorities, genocide, the status of women, missing persons, prisoners of war, family, youth and child welfare, living conditions in underdeveloped areas, housing and town planning, refugees, displaced and stateless persons, narcotic drugs, migration, scientific research and cartography.

Besides the three councils, the General Assembly has six main committees to help it function (First Committee: Political and Security; Second Committee: Economic and Financial; Third Committee: Social, Humanitarian and Cultural; Fourth Committee: Trusteeship, including Non-Self-Governing Territories; Fifth Committee: Administrative and Budgetary; Sixth Committee: Legal). It also has four categories of lesser committees.

Some of the General Assembly's miscellaneous jobs are: electing the nonpermanent members of the Security Council, the members of the Economic and Social Council and the elective members of the Trusteeship Council; appointing the Secretary-General, on recommendation of the Security Council; in independently voting concert with the Security Council electing judges of the International Court of Justice; receiving reports from the Secretary-General, the Security Council and other organs; requesting advisory opinions from the International Court of Justice.

This last body, its fifteen members seated at The Hague, makes final judgment (there's nowhere to appeal) in cases involving UN member nations and also nonmembers under conditions determined by the Assembly on recommendation by the Security Council. Its cases may concern disputes or contending claims only between states, between no lesser disputants. But the Charter provides for its giving legal advisory opinions to various organs of the UN (only the

General Assembly and the Security Council may apply for them direct). Decisions of the Court are enforced, practically speaking, only by its prestige, but this so far has always worked. If it should fail, that is, if one party to a cause should refuse to abide by its decision, the other party could apply to the Security Council, which is authorized to make recommendations or decide on measures to take.

To such disapproving citizens as the taxi driver who wouldn't enter a UN Headquarters building till the UN stopped the Korean War, a standard answer is that the international organization is merely a mechanism that works if we make it, but grinds to a stop if we turn away. In effect, this answer says that member nations and their citizens are responsible for its errors and omissions, not the UN, since the latter is simply a kind of funnel for the will and actions of the former. The International Court of Justice took a quite different legal attitude from this on one notable occasion.

The point on which the Court was asked its opinion was whether or not the UN was legally competent to bring a claim against a government responsible for injury done to one of its agents. The UN agent in the case was Count Bernadotte, murdered in the Israeli area of Palestine in the fall of 1948. In nonlegal terms the question at issue was whether the UN was an entity capable of functioning on its own in the international sphere or merely a combination of nations that individually bore the responsibility for its actions. The opinion handed down said of the UN:

In the opinion of the Court, the Organization was intended to exercise and enjoy, and is in fact exercising and enjoying, functions and rights which can only be explained on the basis of a large measure of international personality and the capacity to operate upon an international plane. It is at present the supreme type of international organization, and it could not carry out the intentions of its founders if it was devoid of international personality. It must be acknowledged that its Members, by entrusting certain functions to it, with the attendant duties and responsibilities, have clothed it with the competence required to enable those functions to be effectively discharged.

"Personality" is a word that we are more accustomed to hearing in connection with psychiatry than with international processes. Perhaps, nevertheless, there is an analogy. The early Freudian approach to establishment of mental health most heavily emphasized the need of understanding personality. The patient lay on a couch and rehashed his intimate life from the womb onward, presumably achieving recovery through understanding of its events. The old view of the way to attain international health was through international understanding: hazily, it was assumed that if every country and its inhabitants knew and understood every other country and its inhabitants, the millennium somehow, without any other stimulation, would appear.

Psychiatrists, of course, still regard understanding (their own of the patient plus his of himself) as the essential first step. But modern members of the profession say action based on the understanding is equally necessary—dynamic effort to replace old bad habits and attitudes and procedures with new good habits and attitudes and procedures. Similarly, international understanding is a basic need, but by itself it's not the panacea you might think, listening to some well-intentioned but old-school workers in the international vineyard. Here, too, dynamic effort is needed for the cure. And it's precisely this that the UN as an entity, or "international personality," daily makes—both on the high legislative-judicial-administrative level of the Assembly, councils, committees and Court just outlined, and on the possibly greater human-interest level of other UN divisions, agencies and people yet to be discussed.

CHAPTER 2

UN-ville

A BRITISH official told of a tanning exhibition he'd seen outside
Rangoon the week before. A young girl spoke reminiscently of
Bangkok. The chance word "Nairobi" from a corner rose above the
cocktail chatter. Two distinguished-looking men were discussing
São Paulo, or some development organization with headquarters
there. "No, I think it was Karachi, in 1949." ". . . on his way to
La Paz . . ." "We'd just left Beirut . . ." Bangalore. Kuwait.
Bizerte. Back to familiar Rome, Paris, Lisbon, Athens. Then swing-
ing wide again to Kuala Lumpur, Reykjavik, Kamchatka, Pango-
Pango, Bokar and Konar . . .

This is the sort of name-dropping that goes on among UN people.
An American transport pilot who thought he had traveled during
World War II would be confused; an ordinary American citizen
feels as if an atlas had dropped on his head.

It is, of course, a natural thing. Sixty nations send their representatives to United Nations, N.Y. UN experts do a great deal of traveling in their work. Even native Americans who stay chained to their
UN desks get so used to communicating with remote associates
that place-names rub off on them. The result for outsiders is a kind
of geographical nightmare. But it's part of life for an inhabitant of
UN-ville.

This is one of the strangest communities in history. To begin
with, it's a town within a city—not just a special area within a city,
like a Chinatown or a financial section or a zoned residential district, but a distinct and treaty-bounded eighteen acres, with separate

laws, a government of its own (aside from its international functions), its own post office, fire department, police force, communications, newspapers, periodicals and book publishing plant, a high-geared kind of "chamber of commerce," retail stores that reflect its unique personality, its own credit union, community planning commission, co-operative, clinic, legal service, library, radio, TV and film production outfits, restaurants, playground and many other things. Its official name, "United Nations, N.Y.," is recognized by post offices everywhere. It has its own flag or emblem, which flies on a level with the flags of all nations. It has a tourist trade that many individual nations would envy. And it has a permanent, tightly knit population of 3,300 whose outlook on life is as singular as the shape its name-dropping takes, as notable as the impression its buildings make on the New York skyline.

No doubt the League of Nations caused a certain amount of commotion moving into Geneva. But the Swiss, as neutrals of long standing, were accustomed to having international conclaves on their hands and probably took the whole enterprise pretty much in stride. League officials, too, for the most part were on familiar ground.

What happened in New York was more drastic. Until Mr. Rockefeller donated the eighteen acres of abattoir-covered land on the bank of the East River, the UN had a vagrant time of it, checking in temporarily at colleges and ex-war plants wherever it could find a room. Then the bulldozers got busy and almost before the Ethiopian delegate could say "Addis Ababa" there was a breath-taking new thirty-eight-story skyscraper for the Secretariat. Soon afterward there was a low-slung Conference Building creeping northward from its base. And finally, in time for the troubled sessions beginning in late 1952, a new and spectacular General Assembly Building, connected with the Conference Building at the north end.

New Yorkers had mixed feelings about the new community. Before its sudden eruption on Manhattan, Americans had been used to the idea, if they ever thought of it at all, that foreign embassies were technically part of the countries which they represented, bits

of foreign territory within the United States. But they were never
so conspicuous as this. Moreover, they were merely bits of single
alien countries. This was an $8,500,000-sized chunk of *international*
territory, owned by sixty nations, and though we were one of them—
in fact a prime mover in the plan—it still seemed strange. Thought-
less Americans complained of "the encroachment of foreigners."

For many of the people of UN-ville, the feeling of strangeness
was undoubtedly more acute. The three main buildings on the
East River are their "downtown," their place of business, and they
have to find living quarters where they can in the city or its suburbs.
This, of course, means that they are exposed to things familiar
enough to us but often confusing or even frightening to them—
subway turnstiles, rush-hour crowds, taxi drivers' conversation,
noise, tabloid newspapers, door-to-door salesmen. As an extreme
example, Indian women found it wiser to wear their native saris
on the streets of New York, though Western dress was more practical in the dust and traffic, because even the diluted anti-Negro
prejudice of the North could be misdirected and embarrassing.

American customs—in tipping, in social conversation (our prone-
ness to ask the direct personal question, for instance), in retail
stores (where courtesy is a rule sometimes overlooked), and in a
host of other categories—are often baffling. But widespread American ignorance of the basic aims and functions of the UN can be a
still greater cause of frustration and dismay.

Language difficulties contribute and there is a natural tendency
for people working at a common task to live where they can see
each other after hours (as successful Madison Avenue advertising
men build their houses in Westport, Connecticut): at any rate,
permanent UN staff members from other countries haven't been
really absorbed in the life of the city. Many live close together in
Parkway Village, a housing development on the outskirts, and there
is a new residential community springing up in Connecticut: that will
be almost entirely inhabited by UN people. Foreign employees
living in scattered apartments and houses tend to gather socially.
There are New York restaurants that attract certain groups: for

example, a Fourteenth Street Russian cabaret at which Scandinavians are regular guests; a mid-town Spanish place that provides entertainment the Latin Americans like.

But the center of things is the group of buildings on the East River.

It might not have been here at all but for the gift of land by Mr. Rockefeller. The United States was the UN's majority choice for the headquarters site, but other cities, especially San Francisco and Philadelphia, were much in the running until his offer. This was an extraordinarily generous thing. It deserves to be remembered, however, that New York City, too, has been generous. To round out the eighteen-acre tract, the City acquired land and deeded it to the UN. Moreover, it deeded streets and waterfront rights and worked out a joint program of improvements with the UN, the City's part of which cost more than $26,000,000.

One difficult and expensive item of New York's contribution was digging a tunnel for a four-lane roadway under the part of First Avenue which runs north and south past the UN site. Once a main artery, First Avenue on the surface here now is limited to local traffic for the convenience of the UN.

For construction of the buildings, Congress made a thirty-year, interest-free loan of $65,000,000 to the UN. An International Board of Design, headed by American architect Wallace K. Harrison, composed the differences of its fifteen different nationalities on the fifty-third try and agreed on plans. This seemed a good augury, since, twenty-five years earlier, it had taken League of Nations architects 577 sets of drawings before they arrived at agreement. The concrete and stone and glass with which the Design Board made substance of its ideas are now a distinctive but increasingly familiar part of the New York scene, an outstanding tourist attraction and, of course, the tightly knit business center of UN denizens.

Most of the employees go to work through the Secretariat Building entrance, near Forty-second Street, but visitors enter at the north end of the General Assembly Building, near Forty-fifth, through any one of seven nickel-bronze doors, the gift of Canada. The great lobby, seventy-five feet high, with its clean-lined hanging galleries, its subdued, almost cathedral-like lighting, makes an immediate, dramatic impression. Visitors feel as if they've stepped into a new and different world. And one hopes they have.

Calling the General Assembly a "town hall of the world" is not a new notion, but it is a valid one, though no town before in America ever boasted a political auditorium of quite such majesty. It's roughly circular in shape, 165 feet long, 115 feet wide and 75 feet from the delegates' floor to the great dome above. Flanking the speakers' rostrum, behind which is the President's podium, gold-leaf-covered vertical strips of fluted wood form screens like stage wings rising from the floor to the dome and covering the walls. Between them, behind the President's podium, a huge United Nations emblem hangs on the wall, surrounded by 68 circular golden shields on which will be placed the coats of arms of member nations. There are 636 seats for delegates on the floor (each mission is entitled to five delegates and five alternates), 270 seats for observers, 234 seats for the press, two tiers of booths for information media around the sides of the hall and accommodation for about 800 visitors. Any significant session easily could fill two or three times that number of guest seats.

It's here, of course, that representatives of the sixty member nations conduct their dramatic debates over war and peace, and other matters that may lead to war or peace.

Since their deliberations are so important to mankind, many people feel that there should be a close religious association. Much of Mrs. Roosevelt's mail contains this or a similar statement: "The UN will never get peace for us till every meeting begins with a prayer." The truth is that General Assembly meetings, at the President's request, *do* always begin with a moment of meditation, which delegates may use to pray in accordance with any of their varying religions. Obviously, it would be impossible to compose a spoken prayer that would be suitable to all the delegates.

Moreover, for more private worship there is in the General Assembly Building a Meditation Room, where many of the delegates, Moslem, Christian, Jewish and other faiths, retire for contemplation and prayer. A triumph of simplicity and nonsectarianism, it's a small room, bare of ornament, draped with a fiber-glass fabric from floor to ceiling. Since corners have objectionable connotations in some faiths, they are rounded by the draperies in the Meditation Room. In place of an altar there stands, upended, toward the front of the room a beautifully polished, 250-year-old section of log believed to have come from the Belgian Congo. There are a dozen or so simple chairs, which may be turned in any direction the worshiper chooses.

Flowers for the Meditation Room are brought daily by the Layman's Movement for a Christian World, which also supplies a visitor's signature book.

Beneath the General Assembly auditorium, on two lower levels, are a large conference room, seven radio studios, four committee rooms, recording rooms and a master control room for the communications system that serves all the Headquarters buildings.

On the first level below the auditorium is a public lobby. This serves as UN-ville's Main Street shopping center. It has a bookshop where all sorts of publications dealing with the UN and its varied activities are sold, along with post cards relating to the UN. It has a gift shop run by the United Nations Co-operative that sells art and handicraft products from many of the member nations. It has a post office from which letters postmarked "United Nations, N.Y." may be mailed. (This really is only a branch of the main UN Post Office, which is under the Secretariat Building.) It has lounges and telephones and checkrooms, and a question-and-answer corner where visitors may and do make the most astounding inquiries. The guided tours start from this lobby.

These guided tours, incidentally, have turned out to be something of a surprise to their sponsor, the American Association for the United Nations. Begun in the fall of 1952 under the direction of Carl Cannon, who learned the business at another sight-seeing attraction for out-of-towners, Radio City, they became far more popular than anyone anticipated. At least half a million customers were a mid-year conservative estimate to pay their dollar apiece during 1953 for a look through the General Assembly Building, plus a running commentary on UN functions and answers to questions by the attractive, multilingual girl guides. Tours were to be doubled in number during the summer absence of delegates, when vacationists come to New York. The chief headache for tour officials came to be complaints from people who had to wait for places on a tour. The officials soon learned that men and women who would stand in line patiently, without a murmur, to get into a baseball game or a movie expected instantaneous attention from a governmental show.

From the lobby under the General Assembly Building a visitor (if he's armed with a pass) walks through a long wide corridor to the Conference Building. Like an iceberg, this structure shows only fifty-five feet above the surface, but is bulkier on the three levels below. Here are the chambers of the Security Council, the Trusteeship Council and the Economic and Social Council—next to the General Assembly the main organs of the UN. All three are the same in size—72 feet wide, 135 feet long and 24 feet high. Partly for the sake of symbolism, these chambers were decorated by artists from the traditionally peace-loving Scandinavian countries: the Security Council by Norwegian Arnstein Arneberg; the Economic and Social Council by Swedish Sven Markelius, and the Trusteeship Council by Danish Finn Juhl.

Under the Council chambers are three large conference halls for the main committees of the General Assembly. These have exits leading to an inviting riverside terrace.

On the upper floors of the building are offices for Secretariat personnel concerned with arranging the conferences. There are also delegates' lounges at either end of the building, a delegates' restaurant, two private dining rooms and a cafeteria for Secretariat workers.

Far below surface is a huge refrigerating plant that air-conditions all the Headquarters buildings. This operation at the UN calls for more flexibility than you might expect, because the inhabitants of UN-ville immigrated from such a wide variety of climates. The engineers have to offer a twelve-degree range of temperatures from which individual offices may make their choices.

Down in the depths, too, are the maintenance workshops of a complete fire-fighting unit, a large printing establishment and document reproduction section, and a garage designed to park 1,500 UN cars.

From the south end of the Conference Building an escalator rises to the main floor of the skyscraper Secretariat Building. This, of course, is the office building of the UN, where some 3,300 men and women work the year around, partly so that in the other two buildings diplomatic members of the sixty national missions may meet and argue in comfort and with all the mechanical aid that modern science and well-trained technicians can bring them. Partly, too, so that other necessary business of the UN, such as giving information to the public, keeping records and maintaining communication with far-flung representatives of the organization, may be conducted.

"But why are so many employees needed?" is a question asked the girl guides by tour members. The answer is the same one given by any experienced Army man when a civilian protests at the ratio of quartermaster and other rear-area personnel to men in combat. The one man with a rifle needs X men to feed him, supply him, care for him in case of sickness or injury, provide him transport, etc., etc. The six hundred delegates on the floor of the General Assembly require similar backing. So do the field workers of the Specialized Agencies, and the special missions sent abroad by the UN to check up on trusteeships, or to try to stop conflicts by negotiation on the spot.

An idler looking up at the narrow side of the Secretariat Building from Forty-second Street spoke cynically to his companion.

"You know why they built it that way?" he asked. "Like a matchbox sitting on one end? They did it so, when they get ready, they can strike a match down the side and the whole thing'll go up in smoke."

It's true that the building does have something of the look of an oversized matchbox on end, but if by "they" the idler meant UN people, he had a wrong idea of their attitude. One supposedly hard-boiled ex-newspaperman gave a hint of their real attitude.

"I'm afraid," he said in a low, half-apologetic tone, looking around to make sure he wasn't overheard, "we're all a little dedicated."

The fountain at the entrance to the Secretariat Building, besides being cool and lovely to look at in New York's hot summers, is a good memory-jogger for dedication. It was a fifty-thousand-dollar gift from the children of the United States and its territories of Alaska, Hawaii, Puerto Rico and the Virgin Islands. On the bed of the shallow pool are wavy alternate bands of black and white pebbles. The black stones were gathered by women and children on the island beaches of Rhodes, and memorialize the UN's role in the pacification of Greece. The gift as a whole commemorates UNICEF's aid to children the world over.

The lobby of the Secretariat Building has little to see but open spaces, banks of elevators and an information booth, to the right of the entrance, where visitors on business are announced and receive their passes to go up into the office areas.

In the elevators a good thing to remember is that regulations forbid smoking. Such regulations exist in many other buildings, but at the UN they are strictly enforced. If you enter an elevator carrying a lighted cigarette you are promptly asked to step out and put it in a receptacle (the floors are too clean for you to consider).

This may seem like laboring a trivial point, but it happens to relate to the whole UN philosophy. Assistant Secretary-General Benjamin V. Cohen, in charge of the Public Information Department, always warns guests with him to put out their cigarettes before entering elevators. But, like other UN officials, he's so used to the strict prohibition that he has to think a moment before explaining the emphasis. Probably the chief reason for the rule is that tobacco offends some staff members on religious grounds. To an outsider, however, the punctiliousness with which the rule is respected goes a little beyond such explanation. It seems more like a grass-roots demonstration of the UN regard for law and order, on every level of importance.

The elevators run up through thirty-eight floors of offices not much different from others you see in New York, except for the variety of nationalities, the greater frequency of fezzes and other costume variations from the American norm. Steel partitions separate the offices, which contain workmanlike simple desks, tables and chairs for the most part, and not nearly the pile of books, pamphlets and documents you might expect in a place that manufactures the printed word on the mass-production scale of the UN. This last is because publications are not permitted to lie around in offices when not in use, but are gathered in strategic storage rooms for call where needed.

Higher officials do go in for leather divans and rugs and other amenities. They also get the best views of the East River, which happens to be an endlessly fascinating waterway, well worth the struggle up the UN hierarchy. On the thirty-eighth floor, where the Secretary-General has his own offices and a small apartment (living room, bedroom, bath, kitchenette; decoration unspectacularly Swedish-modern), the prospect is particularly magnificent. (To some irreverent staff members, at one time during the Korean fighting, an invitation to the top floor was known as "reaching the 38th Parallel.")

Under the Secretary-General there are eight departments sharing the UN's detail work, plus the Technical Assistance Administration and Board. Some visitors have had the idea that the Secretariat Building held offices for the various missions, with the Russians on one floor, the Norwegians on the next and so on (others think it's the place where the UN keeps its eight hundred secretaries and stenographers). Actually, delegations from the sixty member countries do not have offices at UN Headquarters at all; they're scattered about the city in private office buildings. Even the eight Secretariat departments aren't too neatly packaged. Administrative and Financial Services, for example, is on the sixth, seventeenth, thirty-sixth and thirty-seventh floors.

In a general way occupations of UN-ville inhabitants are classified by these eight departments. And the relative amount of work required of each department for the community as a whole is pretty well indicated by the office space it occupies.

Biggest of the departments, occupying 74,509 square feet of space, is the department called Conference and General Services. A brief run-down of its functions will show as quickly as anything could why the Secretariat needs 3,300 employees.

To begin with, it makes all the arrangements and provides all the services for UN meetings and conferences. This means seeing to it, first, that they are properly scheduled not to interfere with other activities. Then it means furnishing translation, interpretation and reproduction of the proceedings, and editing and publishing the journals and official records. It means making transportation arrangements and finding hotel accommodations in connection with the meetings. On a day-to-day basis, not necessarily connected with meetings, it involves purchasing for the Headquarters as a whole, handling mail, cables, telephone and telegraph services, and supervising the files. And, as if this weren't enough, managing the UN buildings and grounds.

Next to Conference and General Services in square footage is the Department of Public Information, with 36,410. The title gives a clear enough idea of this department's objective, but probably not of the complexity of its work. The UN is literally the biggest source of news in the world today. It has hundreds of privately employed journalists regularly covering its activities (the figure goes over a thousand during Assembly sessions). But there are countless other outlets constantly demanding stories and pictures and material for radio broadcasts. So the Department of Public Information (DPI, of course) has half a dozen floors in the building devoted to preparing films, photographs, feature stories, surveys, radio broadcasts. It provides facilities, including liaison, for the press. And it maintains information centers in various parts of the world.

The Department of Economic Affairs, 32,474 square feet, is a hotbed of statistics, providing economic information particularly to the Economic and Social Council, but also to Specialized Agencies and other governmental and nongovernmental organizations.

The Department of Social Affairs has 26,608 square feet of space and a wide range of touchy duties. It prepares meetings, work programs, studies and technical assignments for the Economic and Social Council on problems of human rights, the status of women, health, education, narcotic drugs, cultural activities and refugees. It also provides staff for the General Assembly's Third Committee (Social, Humanitarian and Cultural). It issues publications and helps to write agreements (or conventions, to use the proper term). And it keeps in touch with Specialized Agencies and other organizations concerned with health, education, labor, science, culture and refugees.

The Technical Assistance Administration, though not designated as a department, has 24,974 square feet and supervises the UN program of Technical Assistance for economic development, organizing missions of experts for countries that request them, awarding fellowships and scholarships, and organizing training schools and demonstration centers. It's also responsible for the operation and administration of programs on advisory social welfare functions.

Administrative and Financial Services, 22,692 square feet, has charge of UN personnel, budgetary and fiscal programs, and "maintains relationships" with the Specialized Agencies on such questions. It also has the not always easy task of collecting payments due from member governments. (Beyond a certain point of indebtedness, member governments are liable to lose voting rights. The story is that on one occasion an Oriental member got within ten cents of the deadline.)

The Department of Trusteeship and Information from Non-Self-Governing Territories, 17,183 square feet, serves the Trusteeship Council and other organs of the UN by drafting trusteeship agreements, by examining reports from Administering Authorities in the Trusteeships, by receiving and studying petitions from the people of

Non-Self-Governing Territories, and by making periodic survey visits to the Territories.

The Department of Political and Security Council Affairs, 12,658 square feet, does research and prepares material for the Security Council and its subordinate branches and also for the General Assembly's political committees. The subject matter is anything pertaining to maintenance of peace, including the security aspects of trusteeship agreements for strategic areas. Also in the department's bailiwick is the question of disarmament. It offers advice on peaceful ways to settle disputes and services missions of investigation or conciliation created by the General Assembly or the Security Council.

The Legal Department has only 8,093 square feet, and the Secretary-General's offices, 10,659.

If these departments seem to overlap other organs of the UN in function, such as the councils and committees, it's merely because they are the workhorses for the other organs. They do the research and formulate the material on which the other bodies take action. They do field work and make the practical arrangements under which the other organs operate. And, of course, it's their job to keep the whole UN, as a mechanism, well oiled and smoothly functioning.

Obviously, the higher-level work of most of the departments must be carried on by experts in economics, politics, sociology, health and other specialized fields, who deal in technicalities that wouldn't interest most readers. But a great deal of the lower-echelon activity is fascinating.

Conference and General Services includes some of the more widely interesting activities. Take what most people would call its print shop—the actual title is Internal Reproduction Plant.

Under the direction of Dan DeWalt, veteran of the hectic San Francisco days when the just written Charter had to be reproduced under some of the most trying circumstances ever to confront a printer, this plant (located under the Conference Building) regularly makes a million impressions a day of UN documents and proceedings, of books and pamphlets. Any necessary typesetting is done outside, but five offset machines here turn out the finished records of meetings. Vari-Typers and microfilm cameras are used, too. And batteries of mimeograph machines make copies of proceedings (chuted down from the General Assembly or Council chambers) with phenomenal speed.

The plant has its own artists and cartographers, and the latter have to be the very top men in their trade, because UN maps must be "diplomatically correct." In view of the radical and frequent fluctuations of boundary lines in recent times, even a Rand McNally man might be forgiven for minor errors, but not a UN cartographer. He has sixty sensitive nations ready to pounce if his pen wavers in the slightest degree.

Printing and mimeographing are done in five languages—English, French, Spanish, Russian and Chinese. The first four are simple enough, but Chinese is a special problem, since there is a shortage of Chinese typewriters and, even if there weren't, the nature of its writing defies really rapid mechanical reproduction. There is no alphabet. Printed words are pictographs, with an individual character for each word. A Chinese newspaper has to keep on hand a minimum of 4,500 of these characters. But many of the words used in UN proceedings would not appear in the fonts of a newspaper and certainly not on an ordinary typewriter. Hence, for UN meetings a Chinese calligrapher has to sit in and make a transcript in what, for want of a better word, must be called long hand. As a matter of fact, his speed is greater than any that could be attained on a Chinese typewriter—about 220 characters per minute. The transcript is photographed downstairs in the print shop and reproduced.

The UN Internal Reproduction Plant takes a good deal of pride in the smooth, economical efficiency of its operations. Although it's nonunion (you'll look in vain on UN publications for the familiar little oblong union mark), the 267 employees, who are paid at least union scale, like their jobs well enough to stay with them. After a year and a half with IRP a man is still considered "new."

Probably there is some of the feeling of dedication that runs through the rest of the UN staff, and certainly there is a variety of problems that challenge abilities and keep up interest.

A substantial part of the UN's printing is done outside of IRP, half a million dollars' worth of it outside the United States entirely. When the General Assembly meets away from Headquarters, as it sometimes does—in Paris, for example—the IRP sets up shop right with it. At the last meeting in Paris six IRP supervisors went along to direct the locally hired French printers. Machines were rented in London and Paris and the job went off smoothly enough to permit four of the supervisors to return to the United States after thirty days. DeWalt was impressed with the French printers' eagerness to learn American methods of cutting corners and speeding the work.

His most vivid impressions of UN printing, however, remain the frantic thirty-six hours in San Francisco when his makeshift staff (some members were students enlisted from the University of California across the bay in Berkeley) worked three times around the clock—kept going by Red Cross volunteers who brought coffee and sandwiches, took temperatures and gave first aid. For getting around to the various printing plants (several Chinese newspapers lent facilities) that were used for the rush job of getting out the Charter overnight in five languages, the Army and Navy provided transportation. Someone found an elderly lady in Berkeley who was adept at the fine art of stitching bindings for the presentation copies (she turned out to be wonderfully skillful, but also infuriatingly deliberate).

There were, of course, changes in the original text, then revisions of the changes, then revisions of the revisions, and each time the printers had to reset type. The Chinese newspapers, which had had to cast new characters for the job in the beginning, had to recast them. Typists and mimeograph machines kept up with the changes, just in case all the printing plants blew up at once, and a Chinese calligrapher developed such a swollen wrist from his work (which is done backhand with a sharply bent wrist) that he was helpless for some time afterward.

The final version (okayed at the printing plants by ranking delegates who spoke the five official languages) was printed in duplicate and sent to the Conference for signature in separate police-escorted cars for insurance. Mr. DeWalt carried the second copy himself and by that time was unshaven and disheveled enough to be turned away by the Conference guards. But the first one got through and is now history.

Ceremoniously signed by delegates of all the nations, this copy was to be placed in a leaden casket with a parachute attached and flown to Washington.

A minor footnote: the Charter is written in American-style English, though all other UN documents are in Oxford English, with such spelling as "favour" for our "favor."

Starting at Hunter College with one discarded Navy mimeograph machine, the Internal Reproduction Plant at UN Headquarters alone now manages to run through a thousand tons of paper a year. Before its machines start humming, however, editors must accomplish an extraordinary feat of blue-penciling.

Ahead of the editors, translators—an office full of them for each of the five official languages—put the speeches or resolutions or whatever the material is into the four others besides the original one in which it was presented. Then the five versions go to the editorial section where they are compared, paragraph by paragraph, sentence by sentence and word by word, including footnotes. The five versions must correspond with utter exactitude, down to the last comma.

Unfortunately, literal translations don't always give the precise meaning of originals, and it's exactitude of meaning that is the objective. A classic example (over which there was sharp argument in the UN) is the English word "man." In the general sense, when not used to distinguish a man from a woman, it means to us both men and women. But the literal Spanish translation *"hombre"* means man alone. *Los derechos del hombre* are the rights of men and they exclude women—a point to which Latin women objected vigorously. They won, too, and got a different translation in the Spanish text, the equivalent of "human rights."

At any UN conference or meeting you're likely to hear argument over translation, or at least note the care with which delegates check to be sure translations are correct.

For aid to the editors in particularly difficult cases there is a special small board of last resort called Terminology. It's composed of half a dozen language experts who revise translations on which the editors cannot come to agreement. Terminology also compiles glossaries of technical terms translated into all five official languages. Atomic energy is one of about a hundred subjects covered in the glossaries. For Chinese words the linguists often had to invent atomic pictographs, which must have been a test of imagination.

Translation is one task, and an exacting one. But interpretation, which some people confuse with it, is quite different. While, in the nature of things, it cannot require quite the precision that written transfer of language does, in some ways it's an even more demanding occupation. It's also, for visitors, one of the most interesting activities under the direction of Conference and General Services.

The headset at each seat in the Conference, Council and General Assembly meeting places, as most people know by now, has a dial with six numbers on it. Turning to Number 1 on the dial, the listener hears the speaker straight, in whatever language he's speaking. At Number 2, he hears the speech in English; at 3, French; 4, Russian; 5, Spanish; 6, Chinese.

What he hears in a language other than that being used by the speaker is not direct translation, but a running transfer of the ideas and information being presented. The aim is immediate clarity, and to achieve this a good interpreter needs not only a thorough knowledge of both languages involved but the wit and intelligence to transfer the content of one to the other idiomatically and with the force and flavor of the original. Instantaneously also—just to make it harder.

In the UN Table of Organization there are places for sixty-four interpreters, but at last report twelve vacancies existed, for the reason that competent men and women in this field are harder to find than top-flight nuclear physicists. A well-informed estimate figures the total number able to do the UN work as 120 for the whole world. The UN feels itself lucky to have fifty-two of them. But nowadays when a brash young person phones to ask, "What do I do to learn to be an interpreter?" the courteous brush-off is touched with concern and the thought that something *ought* to be done to train new operatives.

Although the language requirements are a little stringent for most persons who regard themselves as linguists, they aren't too bad. An interpreter must know three languages well enough to reproduce either of two in the third. The requirement does not include work with Chinese. For this language a corresponding knowledge of English only is demanded. But of dozens of applicants who can juggle three languages accurately in ordinary business or social cir-cumstances, it's rare to find one who comes close to UN needs in speed, tact, alertness and understanding. As one of the veteran interpreters pointed out, their motto is "Think," but there's no time to think. Reactions have to be practically automatic—and at the same time, correct.

Interpreters ordinarily work four-hour shifts, but if an important meeting goes on all night, they work all night. Effort is made to assign those with special interests, such as economics, refugee prob-lems, finance, to meetings where their knowledge may be useful.

Of the present staff, eight are women.

A good interpreter loses himself in the job. Even if the ideas expressed are diametrically opposed to those he holds in private life, he transposes them to the other language with as much enthusiasm as the speaker himself. (As one result, radio listeners have been known to telephone and complain that interpreters of Russian speeches were Communists and ought to be fired.) Interpreters are visible behind windows in all the chambers (they find it helpful to see the speakers) and they're often caught copying the very gestures of the orators they're interpreting. At Lake Success, during a speech by the dynamic late Mayor La Guardia, they were so engrossed that all five reached for nonexistent glasses of water when the Mayor quenched his thirst.

On one occasion an interpreter so far lost himself in his work that he forgot everything except his alter ego, the speaker, who happened to be particularly prolix and failing in the organization of his thought. Momentarily missing the drift of his remarks, the interpreter spoke sharply into his microphone, for all to hear: "I don't understand you." Since no one else did either, the lapse was greeted with sympathetic laughter.

Chinese makes for varied difficulties. On one occasion it wasn't the language itself but the accent applied to English that caused trouble. A Chinese dignitary insisted on addressing a meeting in English. His delivery was so hard to understand, however, that the interpreters found the double task of figuring out what he meant and translating it simultaneously into the other languages altogether beyond their powers. As a quick solution they got a woman interpreter to translate the Chinese English into English English and from there they happily took it into French, Spanish, Russian and Chinese itself, where it should have started. They were, of course, a few seconds behind in their interpreting, but all would have been well if the orator hadn't been so proud of his speech that he asked for a recording. The woman's voice that appeared on it deeply hurt his feelings and required a high degree of professional diplomacy, fortunately available, to explain.

Another time, in Paris, the Russian Vishinsky was making a speech at a closed meeting. Usually when the public is excluded recording is omitted, but Vishinsky particularly asked for it, and the technicians set up the apparatus. Unaccountably, however, they attached wires backward or slipped up in some other way. What should have been recorded from the Number 1 slot on the dial, the speech as he made it, came out of Number 6 instead. On the playback later, it was an unnerving experience for Mr. Vishinsky to hear himself speaking in Chinese. Shamefacedly the interpreters offered to run the discourse back through English (as would have been necessary from the Chinese) into the original Russian, but he told them not to bother—conceivably afraid it might all end up in Ubangi.

The kind of interpretation heard through the headsets from the interpreters' soundproof booths is known as "simultaneous." It's the rule in most UN meetings. Only in the Security Council and the Disarmament Commission, where misinterpretation is liable to involve special dangers, is a second system, called "consecutive interpretation," also used. During a speech simultaneous interpreters present it in the usual way, in English, French, Spanish, Russian and Chinese. But after it's finished the consecutive interpreters, whose primary qualification for the job is evidently total recall, rise and repeat what the speaker said, in French and English, miraculously reproducing gestures, emphasis and sometimes even intonation.

These carefully worked out methods of communicating what is said on the floor of the General Assembly, the council chambers and committee rooms in all the five official languages include wiring not only to seats in the various meeting places, but also to the offices of high UN officials in the Secretariat Building, who can tune in via a gadget called the MX on whatever discussion they wish, whenever they wish, in any of the languages they wish.

Accurate translation and interpretation are a conspicuous necessity for effective international effort. The UN's techniques are interesting from the "gadget" point of view, but also significant as indications of the way modern technology can help clear the way to understanding. Of course, the five official languages are not by any means native to all the delegates, most of whom are forced to carry on business in tongues that are foreign to them. But within practical limitations the UN does quite a linguistic job. American visitors are even struck by the trivial fact that direction signs throughout the Headquarters buildings are in two languages, French and English ("Pull" and "Tirez" on the doors) and will be more so when the "officializing" of Spanish to a first-place position requires adding a third language.

On the more prosaic level of mail, telephones and telegraph, Conference and General Services does a large-scale communications business—large enough to necessitate the full-time services of a telephone company liaison officer in that category. UN-ville, as you might expect, is one of the world's most dedicated users of Alexander Graham Bell's invention, particularly long distance.

The UN switchboard is open twenty-four hours a day, 365 days in the year. Its 3,260 telephone installations require the services of twenty operators, including supervisors. Conference and General Services makes its own engineering plans for telephone operations, tells the telephone company what it wants, and gets it. One item is the special jacks that can be plugged in by press and radio representatives for direct communication from the council chambers and General Assembly hall to news rooms outside.

Connected with the switchboard is an information bureau. If you want to know the date of the next Committee Four meeting or the name of the head delegate from Mexico, you will be switched to information and one of the six girls on duty there will give you an answer in no time. Ingenious rotary lists of facts help speed their work. But if your question goes beyond the strictly factual, if it's at all controversial or dependent on opinion, you're given over to the UN agency or organ most closely concerned. As a farfetched example, if you call irately to ask why Soviet Russia isn't thrown out of the UN, you may get a sobering, well-documented explanation from an official of the Security Council itself.

Mail comes into UN-ville at the rate of about four thousand letters a day. It's opened and looked at by three men who have knowledge of half a dozen languages, who route it to the proper offices for response. (General letters from the public are answered by a correspondence section set up for the purpose.)

Distribution of the letters and periodicals and small packages that come in is made via dumb-waiters that run up shafts through the thirty-eight stories of the Secretariat Building—probably the tallest dumb-waiters in the world—and then by messenger to the individual offices. Additional magazines and newspapers arrive by underground pneumatic tube from the Library, which receives a staggering volume of publications from all over the world. (The Library is a small, six-story building, not included in the Design Board's plans for UN Headquarters but purchased already built from the City. It's about fifty yards from the Secretariat Building, toward First Avenue.)

Outgoing correspondence handled by the mail room amounts to about five thousand letters a day. A considerable portion of the important letters goes by diplomatic pouch; there are thirty pouch centers in regular use as destinations. By emphasizing the fact that this method of communication avoids the censorship imposed in various places on cable and radio transmissions, or at least the lack of privacy, the mail room has succeeded in reducing the flow of cablegrams to an economical level of about 170 outgoing and incoming messages a day. In addition, there is a direct circuit to Geneva open for about one hour daily. From there messages are distributed to other points in Europe. But for the most part, ordinary commercial channels are used for wire and radio communication.

Conference and General Services also is responsible for all filing of UN correspondence and documents. The archives alone, for inactive documents and letters, take up 11,000 cubic feet of space.

Of 1,422 staff members employed by Conference and General Services, 363 are occupied in Buildings Management Service. This division of the department oversees the housekeeping procedures, takes care of the grounds, runs the fire department and the corps of guards, repairs the furniture, operates an architectural drafting room (with three draftsmen) to design changes in office space, lighting, air-conditioning arrangements and such interior matters, and does all kinds of other odd jobs. Under its authority there's even a "take your own picture" machine, like those at amusement parks, for the use of traveling UN staff members who need passport pictures and all the others who need pictures for their UN passes.

The carpenter shop keeps six men busy maintaining furniture and making more or less unpurchasable, unstandardized objects such as temporary booths for the guards. There are also plumbing, sheet metal and air-conditioning repair shops.

The fire department, with its station in the third basement of the Conference Building, is a particular pet of Conference and General Service. It has ultramodern equipment and a thoroughly trained force of fifteen men, on duty at all times in shifts of three. (The UN guards, too, are trained in fire-fighting, and maintenance men as well, but the firemen would be in command if a fire broke out.) Since the UN buildings were constructed with practically every conceivable safeguard against burning, the most serious blazes so far have come from cigarettes carelessly tossed in wastebaskets, and have stopped there, with no damage to anything except discarded papers. Nevertheless, the firemen keep on the alert, ready for any emergency, their best hope for excitement being the interior designers, who often oppose the use of fire-resistant materials in their schemes of decoration. If a real conflagration ever occurred, all the resources of the New York City Fire Department would be available.

The UN guards, 140 of them, are another trim and well-trained group without much outlet for their indicated talents. Only three are armed, plain-clothes men who accompany personnel carrying money (people connected with the guided tours or cafeteria, for example). Just as no real fire has ever happened, however, no real robbery attempt has come along to test the capacity of the guards. No violence of any sort, at the present Headquarters, and guards spend most of their time giving courteous directions. But officials go on knocking wood and urging the force to keep on the alert. Both firemen and guards make a minor career of *preventing* fires and accidents, such as slipping and falling. Their job is promoting safety, rather than checking the damage of crime or negligence.

(Outside the Headquarters buildings proper, in the unoccupied area to the north, the UN has built a playground which City youngsters having no connection with the UN are permitted to use. The guard assigned to keep peace here has a job on his hands that would give pause to the career peacemakers in the General As-

ST PAUL
PUBLIC LIBRARY

sembly and Security Council to the south. Being a New York father himself, he manages.)

If a crime *should* be committed within the Headquarters district, and the culprit apprehended by the barehanded guards, he would be turned over to City police, unless it happened to be a Federal offense, in which case, presumably, the FBI or Postal detectives, or whatever the proper authorities were for the transgression, would be given charge. Under the terms of the agreement with the United States which governs UN operations on American soil, the Headquarters district is inviolable to Federal, state or local officers, except by UN consent. However, unless UN regulations conflict (in which unlikely cases they would have precedence over national or local ordinances), domestic statutes must be observed, and a purse-snatcher has as good a chance of winding up in the Tombs from the General Assembly Building lobby as he does from Times Square.

Incidentally, the U.S.-UN agreement for the Headquarters district carefully specifies that services like electricity, water, gas, post, telephone, telegraph, transportation, drainage, collection of refuse, fire protection and snow removal must be supplied to the UN on equitable terms, with its needs treated as equal to those of "essential agencies of the Government of the United States." Since the Government of the United States is required to "take steps accordingly to ensure that the work of the United Nations is not prejudiced," it seems clear that having the gas or phone cut off is not one of the Secretary-General's major worries.

The 5,400 windows which let so much symbolic light into the Secretariat Building (and by a special process of manufacture filter out heat) are not only a distinguishing mark that never fails to catch the eye of visitors, but also quite a cleaning chore. Like a number of other housekeeping tasks and building services, the cleaning is done under contract on a fixed fee basis with a private American firm, which supplies nine men to polish the year around. There are 1,200 additional windows in the other Headquarters buildings and green glass spandrels between the windows of the Secretariat Building that have to be cleaned, too. The men keep busy.

Inside cleaning is another contract job, with 54 mops going during the day and 140 at night. The one and a half miles of elevator shaftways throughout Headquarters that provide 250 miles of elevator transportation per day are under the jurisdiction of girl operators who also are supplied by outside contract. Radio electricians, sidewalk, road and grounds keepers and exterminators all work on this basis, too. The exterminators, by the way, inherited a rodent-and-roach problem from Mr. Rockefeller's previous bovine tenants that they would willingly return.

Contract workers likewise clean the filters and inject anticorrosive into other parts of the air-conditioning system. The lawns (like putting greens), gardens and 440 trees that beautify the grounds are still under guarantee by the gardening outfit that set them up, but probably will be cared for under contract later.

Similarly, the dining room and cafeteria are operated by employees of a hotel chain. The cafeteria, on which the UN spent $300,000 for equipment, serves 85,000 customers a month; the dining room, 21,000 for lunch only. Conference and General Services says what food is to be served and names the price range.

Employing the contract system is regarded as cheaper and more efficient than hiring people directly to do such work, involving, as that would, the expense of paying for supervision and the finding of extra office space for the supervisors. The thirty-eight-story Secretariat Building, originally planned for forty-two stories, already is somewhat strained at the seams and visiting officials would have a time finding temporary parking space for their papers if it weren't for the fact that permanent occupants of offices do so much traveling.

For parking cars the department has a subterranean garage that was intended to take care of 1,500 cars for delegates, UN employees and people coming to Headquarters on business. Shortage of room elsewhere in the building has cut into its capacity, however, the storage space that was meant for Chevrolets being occupied by supplies. The service station in the garage is not a department function; it's run by the UN Co-operative.

To save employee time and elevator use going to the cafeteria, there are portable wagons that trundle through the Secretariat Building, mornings and afternoons, carrying coffee, rolls and other tidbits. This is a logical and pleasant service, bringing the refreshment to the customer. But in the lounges, if you want a drink, you go to the bar yourself and bring it back to your table. This wastes no official working time or elevator space.

The item labeled "Purchasing and Transportation" among Conference and General Services duties covers such a multitude of things that an officer of the department gets irascible if he's asked general questions about it, and you can't altogether blame him. American businessmen, however, and particularly New York businessmen, beam when the subject comes up. In the light of items like $254,000 for the telephone company; $614,000 for public utilities; $200,000 for office fixtures; $130,000 for pencils, pens, inks and envelopes; or $300,000 for mimeograph materials such as paper, stencils and chemicals, you can't blame them either.

A *New York Times* study of the 1953 UN budget gave an over-all figure of $4,000,000 for "common services," which included the contract maintenance work of cleaning, electrical work and elevator operation. In addition, Conference and General Services foresaw a bill of more than $2,000,000 for travel by delegates and Secretariat personnel on special missions, half of which would go to American transportation companies.

(These *Times* figures, incidentally, were only part of an article showing how much in dollars and cents the United States got out of the UN establishment in New York. Although citizens have been known to complain about the $15,500,000 the U.S. Treasury pays as our share of the regular UN budget, the measurable cash money spent by the UN, its staff and its delegations in this country is at least $37,000,000. Moreover, replacement of slaughterhouses with the magnificent UN Headquarters buildings has doubled or tripled real estate values in the City area, and increased tax revenue.)

Another of the Secretary-General's departments that has more than technical interest is Public Information, second in size to Conference and General Services with 291 staff members. In effect, it's UN-ville's Chamber of Commerce.

The UN, as has been said before, is the greatest single source of news in the world today. This is demonstrably true by any standard you choose for measurement—quantity, importance, universality of interest.

Normally, there are about three hundred privately employed reporters accredited to the UN, with fifty or sixty daily newspapers represented. At what have lately been the infrequent meetings of the Security Council (though delegates are required to stand by at all times in case one should be called) eight or nine hundred correspondents make their appearance. At the 1951 General Assembly in Paris, two thousand foregathered.

Radio coverage of UN activities is, if anything, even more impressive, with news and feature material on the air twenty-two hours a day, in twenty-five or twenty-six different languages. Stations in the United States alone that carry programs about the UN number fourteen hundred and not a cent is paid for time. Short-wave transmitters are rented for news broadcasting to other parts of the world, and it's a UN boast that these news programs are never "jammed."

Since most member states rebroadcast its programs, the UN, DPI claims, has probably the biggest loyal radio audience in the world at the lowest cost. Special broadcasts at times are estimated to have more than 500,000,000 listeners. For the enthusiasm of the audience officials cite such cases as Claudia Cruz, "Sweetheart of the Philippines," who broadcasts UN news on every station in every Philippine network and whose followers include thousands of Filipinos who gather at communal listening posts in the remote jungles or on the towering mountains, wherever a radio receiver can be found.

Assistant Secretary-General Benjamin V. Cohen, head of Public Information, says the UN was the first major user of television, with a program called "UN Casebook." Certainly, the new medium has given dramatic presentation to the UN picture. And expanded plans for use of films on TV will demonstrate the UN's activities to more and more millions as television develops.

There are also films to be shown on screens not of the television variety, there are filmstrips and other visual materials, and there are news services and news feature services and books and pamphlets.

Much of the department's work in spreading information to the public is stage-managing. For headline news its function is to provide the best facilities possible for working newspapermen and the radio press at all conferences. Newsreels and TV get the same attention. Beyond that, Press Services facilitates any interviews writers may wish for feature stories, magazine articles or books, arranges press conferences and helps to furnish background material.

But Public Information's own production of copy and photographs and other material is of formidable proportions. To begin with, it covers in the most objective style it can manage all the activities of the UN at Headquarters. The press releases stemming from this comprehensive coverage total between three and four thousand a year and are aimed at the needs of: (1) the press and radio correspondents covering the UN; (2) all the other media services of the Department of Public Information; and (3) Information Centers scattered about the world (seventeen of them overseas).

For these releases and the texts of important documents and resolutions and the like, a teletype service is available, on a subscription basis, to press associations, newspaper, radio and delegation offices.

Because many smaller newspapers, particularly weeklies, here and abroad, cannot afford commercial coverage of the UN and still are eager for authentic information, the Department has a printed and illustrated news feature service in several languages which is sent, by request only, to several thousand papers in forty different countries.

A Daily Report and Weekly Summary are sent to Information Centers and UN missions in various parts of the world. There is also limited radio service to the same recipients.

Besides, the department is responsible for the semimonthly *United Nations Bulletin*, the monthly *United Nations Reporter* and the annual *Yearbook of the United Nations* and *Everyman's United Nations*.

The "market" for information from the department is clearly enormous. If the budget permitted, many times the present amount of production could be easily absorbed—but the budget does not permit. Therefore, outside help has been asked and a great deal given. The UN cannot afford much, for instance, in the way of making films. But it can give independent movie producers collaboration on material and in the process of production, and does just that. Similarly, commercial picture syndicates and national information services help in the expensive distribution of photographs.

The two thousand Non-Governmental Organizations associated with the UN (the International Chamber of Commerce, International Confederation of Free Trade Unions, Y.M.C.A., etc.) are a particularly valuable means of disseminating information. Many have accredited observers at UN Headquarters who send reports directly to their organizations. At one time they all received basic documentation and other information directly from the department, but now, for reasons of economy, the Information Centers have been made responsible for keeping them up-to-date.

These Non-Governmental Organizations have a high absorption point for speeches, and not only by their own members. The Department of Public Information gets close to a thousand requests a year for speakers. Somewhat more than half of these are granted by Secretariat officials or other UN dignitaries, and the rest are referred to the Voluntary Correspondent Speakers' Units or other outside sources of lectures on the UN.

Assistant Secretary-General Cohen and Mrs. Dorothy Lewis, head of the radio division, are such indefatigable and able platform performers, however, that they could probably manage by themselves, if necessary. As information experts, they are in particular demand, and it's part of their function to go along with as many requests as is physically possible.

Administrative and Financial Services, besides drawing up budgets and handling the UN's expenses (including collecting the wherewithal to pay them), deals with the question of personnel. There are about 3,300 regular employees of the UN in New York, 600 or 700 at Geneva and others scattered around the world on political, economic and cultural missions, and in Information Centers. About 800 of the New York 3,300 are stenographers and typists, another 800 clerks. Nearly all of these 1,600 are hired locally, on the normal basis of skill and experience.

In the more specialized jobs—the economists, statisticians, lawyers, etc.—other considerations may enter. An effort is made to distribute the work equitably among member nations when they want it for their nationals—which not all of them do. Soviet Russia, for example, though suspected by some Americans of using the UN as a base for information-gathering activities, has been reluctant indeed to supply needed technical help, explaining that too many of its best technicians had been killed in World War II. Of something like 120 or 130 jobs the UN wanted Russians to fill in the Secretariat, only 20 were filled.

The international aspects of staffing are Personnel's chief problem, and not necessarily from the angle of deciding on quotas for the various member nations. A particular headache is that in choosing among applicants from far countries reliance must be placed on the judgment of third persons.

A special task of Personnel is staffing the various missions (there were eight in the field at last count) serving the General Assembly, the Security Council and the Trusteeship Council overseas. Except for specialists added from outside for specific problems and manual and clerical help hired locally, these missions are made up of permanent UN staff members.

The Headquarters guards, firemen and 150 to 160 manual workers (carpenters, locksmiths, plumbers, sheet metal workers, furniture repair men and the like) are processed through Personnel. But not the elevator operators, the cleaning people, exterminators, maintenance and radio electricians, sidewalk and road keepers—all of whom work under contract arrangements and are hired by their own outside bosses.

UN salaries are not munificent. They range from the beginning gross of a messenger, $2,230 (after deductions, a net $1,900), to the Secretary-General's $33,000 with added allowance of $20,000. (Deductions, incidentally, are for the benefit of American employees, who are the only nationals working for the UN not exempt from income tax; money coming out of the deduction fund goes to pay their taxes, thus equalizing rates of compensation among all personnel.) Very few salaries get to the $10,000 level, and probably most medium-grade staff members receive less than they would in comparable private American employment.

Vacations are another matter, however. Everyone is entitled to six weeks' leave with pay, and these annual holidays may be accumulated up to a total of sixty working days. To most Americans, accustomed though they are to fairly generous vacation privileges, this sounds lavish. But, aside from the fact that the UN likes to set an example in working conditions, there are a couple of very practical justifications.

For one thing, some staff members live on the other side of the globe and, though travel time is not counted in vacations, the trip for two weeks would be hardly worth the effort. If you protest that they could take their vacations closer to UN-ville, the answer is that the UN wants them to go home, because as working members of the organization they advertise its aims and increase its prestige more than anything else could in their own birthplaces. This is one reason why the UN pays for their transportation.

For the second thing, six-weeks vacations are not so costly to the UN as they might be to private industry, because there are no budget provisions to take up the added work load made by such employee absences. It's simply divided as best the office heads can do among nonvacationing employees.

In addition to salary, UN employees receive a $200 annual allowance for each child under eighteen (under twenty-one if the boy or girl is still in school full time, or is totally disabled). And for social security there is a United Nations Joint Staff Pension Fund, plus a system of health protection, sick leave and maternity leave, and "reasonable compensation in the event of illness, accident or death attributable to the performance of official duties on behalf of the United Nations."

The wave of loyalty investigations and fear for national security stirred up within the United States in recent years has affected American personnel in the UN. One prominent staff member committed suicide in what was believed to be despair over the attitude of Congress and a large section of the American people. Others resigned or lost their jobs as a result of suspicion that they had been connected with various organizations labeled as subversive. The feeling of uncertainty among the remainder that developed as a consequence found pointed expression in a not very funny joke.

A high American official, according to this story, entered the Secretariat Building and was stopped by a new guard who didn't recognize him.

"Do you work here?" the guard asked.

"I don't know," replied the high official. "I did last week, but I just got back from London, and haven't found out yet!"

There have been ticklish questions at issue between the UN and the United States Government over the loyalty screening of American personnel. These may take a good deal of time to answer to the satisfaction of both parties, since they relate to delicate balances of jurisdiction, authority and "face." The Secretary-General and other UN leaders are inclined to have confidence in their own judgment for selecting staff members (with appropriate background help from the proper governmental agencies that are willing to supply it). But they also earnestly want the American people to have a better understanding of the nature of the loyalty that's required of UN staff members. This is clearly outlined in the oath or declaration which each staff member is obliged to make. Its text:

I solemnly swear (undertake, affirm, promise) to exercise in all loyalty, discretion and conscience the functions entrusted to me as an international civil servant of the United Nations, to discharge these functions and regulate my conduct with the interests of the United Nations only in view, and not to seek or accept instructions in regard to the performance of my duties from any government or other authority external to the Organization.

This oath (or affirmation if the employee's religion forbids oaths) is taken before the Secretary-General, or an authorized deputy. It's only one of thousands of ceremonies and duties that are the lot of the Secretariat's head man.

The Secretary-General (Trygve Lie for so long that he began to seem irreplaceable; now Dag Hammarskjold—who doesn't mind if it's pronounced "Hammershield") is a top political figure in the UN, with a right stipulated in the Charter to bring any matter he considers a threat to peace before the Security Council and a duty to notify the General Assembly when the Security Council ceases to consider such matters. This gives him more power than may be apparent.

The Secretary-General, partly because of the relative permanence of his position (unlike the President of the General Assembly who changes each year, he has no set term of office provided in the Charter) and partly because of his widely ramified authority over the whole UN organization, tends to become its chief personality, its embodiment and its spokesman to the world.

He also has the more mundane and not less burdensome task of being the Secretariat's chief administrator. Under him are the already described eight regular departments of the Secretariat and the Technical Assistance Administration and Board. One of the four sections of his Executive Office deals with the Specialized Agencies, such as UNESCO, the World Health Organization and the International Labour Organisation, and the co-ordination of their activities. The other three are the Office of the Executive Assistant to the Secretary-General, the General Assembly Affairs and Administrative Section, and the Protocol and Liaison Section.

Under the Executive Assistant, among other things, is UN-ville's Library.

This is a six-story structure standing about fifty yards west of the Secretariat Building. It was intended originally for the New York City Housing Authority, but the UN bought it while still under construction for $1,400,000.

One of the first things an outsider notices with pleasure about the UN Library is that he may smoke in it. He's allowed to move around in the stacks at will, directed to the proper sections by co-operative and knowing librarians. The small tables provide good working space.

Beginning at Hunter College in 1946 with a small reference collection, the Library now has about 150,000 volumes. It receives about 2,000 periodicals and adds about 1,350 items a year to its pamphlet file. It has a collection of 50,000 government documents, including all those of the U.S. State Department, and receives about 30,000 new official gazettes and documents each year. It has copies of the laws and statutes of UN member nations, and copies of all UN and Specialized Agency documents. It has a collection of 40,-000 maps. Its main reference room has 10,000 volumes, including dictionaries and encyclopedias in many languages, and microfilm editions of the *New York Times*, the Russian *Izvestia* and the London *Times*. Its Woodrow Wilson Memorial Library contains about 19,000 volumes of documents and publications by and about the League of Nations. (None of the 400,000 books from the League of Nations Library, now known as the UN Geneva Library, is in New York; they all remain in Switzerland.)

In addition, the UN Library has a continuing arrangement with the New York Public Library to borrow any of its books, including reference material and volumes from special collections. Books are picked up and delivered daily by UN chauffeurs.

The UN Library has four branches within the Secretariat Building serving the Political and Security Council Affairs, Trusteeship, Legal, and Economic and Social Affairs departments.

It loans more than 50,000 books, documents and periodicals a year, routes 117,000 documents and periodicals from departmental libraries to offices and individuals, and borrows from other libraries about 6,500 books annually.

Documents, almost always as gifts, are received from fifty-two member countries, seventy Trust and Non-Self-Governing Territories and twenty nonmember nations. Many private organizations and institutions also send material, two-thirds of it gratuitously.

There are, you will have noticed, no whodunits mentioned, no historical novels, no how-to-be-happy tracts, no volumes of poetry. This is still the business district of UN-ville and the business is the sober one of world improvement, not escape.

The same restriction of subject matter applies to the retail bookshop on UN-ville's Main Street, the lobby on the first lower level of the General Assembly Building. This is chiefly an outlet for UN publications, which number close to three hundred a year, not counting translations or periodicals, though it also sells books pertaining to the UN which are published commercially. (The UN is one of the largest book publishers on earth, with manufacturing facilities scattered all over the world and more than a hundred sales agents, such as Columbia University Press in this country, peddling its products everywhere that people read.)

An average of thirteen hundred customers patronize the Bookshop daily, and it's open every day in the week, including all holidays except Christmas. Many drop in just for UN post cards, but a great many others are interested in reading about the UN as well as seeing it. *Your United Nations*, a souvenir guidebook that is photographically excellent and packs in a generous assortment of pertinent facts about the organization, quickly sold fifty thousand copies and was reprinted in a new edition of forty thousand. This is a sample of the general interest.

Business and professional people, no matter what their political attitude is toward the UN, find its specialized publications concretely valuable and are taking a steadily increasing interest in the titles that appear on the Bookshop's shelves. Studies on international tax agreements, on world economic trends, on tariff agreements, on agricultural production, on foreign investments, on public health, on any number of other technical matters are within the capacity of the UN when no other organization has the facilities to make them. The published results find avid buyers among practical people in sixty-three countries, including the United States, and though most prices are low, UN books are expected to do a $300,000 business in 1954.

The Bookshop itself is an appendage of the Public Information Department, through its Sales and Circulation Division.

If the Bookshop on UN-ville's Main Street confines itself to serious-minded merchandise, the near-by Gift Shop compensates with a colorful and by comparison frivolous assortment of goods for sale. Thin silk Indian scarves, Scandinavian pewter pitchers, bric-a-brac and ceramics and jewelry from a wide variety of sources, and any number of other imported articles decorate its counters and shelves—but only momentarily. Ever since its opening in the fall of 1952 (Mrs. Roosevelt officiated at the ceremony), the Gift Shop has looked like a bargain sale at Macy's, and its executive director, Mary Dean, herself a buyer-graduate of the famous department store, as well as a teacher of arts and crafts, has been hard put to it to keep it stocked.

Merchandise of the Gift Shop comes from various member nations of the UN. The quantity of each item sold is too small to interest large-scale commercial retailers, but through the Gift Shop the arts and crafts of countries whose wares were previously unknown to Americans receive an introduction in favorable surroundings. The sales, though relatively minor in dollar volume, do stimulate the artists and craftsmen of distant and underdeveloped countries. And this is a major purpose of the undertaking.

As an example of why such indigenous arts and crafts need stimulation, the American economic adviser to Ethiopia some years ago became fascinated by the beautiful primitive paintings on thin goatskin he saw in Addis Ababa. He was sure his own countrymen would regard them with the same favor and that a profitable American market could be set up for the Ethiopian artists, whose work was selling at home for a matter of pennies. When he took his idea to the Government, however, he met resistance that no amount of argument could overcome. The Government felt that the primitives were too primitive, an improper advertisement for the level of Ethiopian culture and not to be exported. The economic adviser even had to use caution getting his personal collection of the paintings out of the country when he left.

The point is, of course, that where an individual failed in such a case, with only nebulous commercial outlets in mind, an organization like the Gift Shop, with a widespread reputation for high cultural standards and the weight of UN prestige behind it, easily could override the Government's objections. And everyone would be happier for it—artists, Government, Gift Shop and picture buyer.

The Gift Shop is an operation of the UN Co-operative, which also runs the service station in the UN garage and has tried, but failed, to be given charge of the cafeteria.

The idea of the Co-op came up at a cocktail party back in 1947 when the UN was at Lake Success. Staff members were having mechanical trouble with prewar cars, and financial and other sorts of trouble with the mechanics they hired to do repairs. Complaints over the situation were practically the whole content of the cocktail conversation until someone suggested the co-operative solution. It was enthusiastically agreed upon and the founders pledged $2,500 to start their venture. Incorporated under Washington, D.C., statutes, the Co-op made its first deal with the Sinclair Oil Company for gas and oil, and set up a service station near the Sperry plant, where the UN then had temporary quarters.

In the present UN garage the Co-op service station sells no gasoline, because safety regulations forbid it. But it still sells oil, and three mechanics and a washman attend to the cleanliness and internal health of UN-connected cars. No body work is done.

Nowadays, there are 750 members of the Co-op. Its stock sells at ten dollars a share, the minimum purchase being one share, the maximum, fifty. It regularly pays the legal limit in dividends, 4 per cent. Members and nonmembers alike save receipts on their service station payments, their Gift Shop and Bookshop purchases. At the end of each fiscal year, after the annual meeting, when profits have been totted up, members get a cash rebate on their year's buying, usually 10 per cent. Nonmembers may apply this percentage of their purchases only against the price of membership stock.

Co-op membership is open to Secretariat personnel, to the delegation staffs of member nations and to the representatives of nongovernmental organizations who regularly consult on or observe UN activities.

Another busy spot on UN-ville's Main Street, right outside the Bookshop, is a branch of the UN Post Office, where visitors may buy UN stamps and mail letters postmarked "United Nations, N. Y." Contrary to some opinion, this branch and the main UN Post Office under the Secretariat Building are not run by the UN, but by members of the United States Post Office Department. The printing of UN stamps is an expense of the international organization, but revenue from their sale-for-use goes to the United States. Only philatelic profits accrue to the UN.

Besides document sales, stamps are the one source of independent income owned by the UN, all the rest of its funds being contributions from member governments. As a rare source of independent income, they engender a paternal pride and concern far greater than the dollar proceeds would seem on the surface to warrant—an estimated net for 1953 of $400,000. It may strike Americans as odd that an organization of sixty great nations, with a modest over-all annual budget, including the Specialized Agencies and the Expanded Technical Assistance Program, of only a hundred million or so, should bother itself about a tiny sum like $400,000. Our Congress spends scores of billions a year without excessive anxiety over their origin. The difference, no doubt, is that Congress also has the right to tax, whereas the Secretary-General can merely propose a budget, with contributions to meet it proportioned as fairly as he knows how among the member nations—then hope that they deliver.

At any rate, the philatelic shop near the main Post Office does make money for the UN, selling UN stamps, not for mailing use, but for collectors. The only other reasonably immediate prospect the UN has in the way of profit-making is the guided tours. Although these were set up by the private American Association for the

United Nations, and at last reports were still paying back the substantial loan on which they started business (girl guide uniforms cost $125 apiece), the idea has been eventually to turn the proceeds over to the UN General Fund.

For the financial needs of UN individuals there is a Credit Union, started in 1948 largely through the inspiration of Victor Kwong, Administrative Officer in the Department of Trusteeship and Information from Non-Self-Governing Territories, and long-time foe of sharp commercial small-loan practices.

The Credit Union began with thirteen charter members, each of whom chipped in $1.75. It grew and the shares became more valuable. There are now about 1,725 active accounts, meaning members, and a share costs $25, plus a 25¢ membership fee. The reason for its growth is plainly apparent in a comparison of its interest rates with those of commercial institutions. (On a $500 unsecured personal loan repaid within a year the charge by a conservative New York bank—not a loan shark—would be somewhere between $36.75 and $58.90; the charge by the Credit Union would be $24.24.)

On savings accounts the Credit Union pays 3.8 per cent interest. It will accept up to $50 a month in deposits. The maximum investment permitted is $3,000.

Admittedly, UN staff members from far countries have a hard time adjusting themselves to life in New York. Most of them want to learn how we live, to share in our social life, to get out of the strict UN orbit occasionally and experience for themselves the things that are familiar to Americans. But language difficulties, long hours of work and lack of opening acquaintanceships tend to stand in the way.

Back in 1948 the UN Volunteer Services was organized to do whatever was possible to meet this social problem. Under the direction of Miss Aroos Benneyan, its most successful venture has been a scheme for persuading American families to invite UN individuals, families or groups for visits in their homes. So far such visits have been made in seventeen states, for periods varying from three days to three weeks, and the results have been remarkably free of disaster. Both hosts and guests have been surprised by the rapid establishment of mutual understanding. The visits often have led to lasting friendships and to a marked broadening of social life for the UN people.

One unlikely-sounding holiday that came off well was a Christmas visit by an Iranian family of four to a Scarsdale, New York, home. It was the Middle-Easterners' first exposure to an American Christmas, but they joined in the tree-trimming and other ceremonies, and everyone had a fine time.

Communities usually take to the idea and give it a good deal of local publicity. At Skidmore, Pennsylvania, the mayor greeted a party of UN visitors, the Chamber of Commerce treated them to a sight-seeing tour, and the various families among whom they were split up for housing had them join in our outlandish customs for celebrating Halloween. It was a weekend and some unusually intelligent person supervising the local arrangements handled the question of churchgoing (none of the party was Christian) with excellent taste. On Saturday night each family invited its guests to attend church the next morning, but left the choice very clearly up to the UN visitors, without any approval or disapproval either way. This had the good effect of creating a feeling of "belonging" without any sense of coercion.

The UN people pay for their own transportation on such jaunts (Volunteer Services arranges it), and for incidentals, but otherwise they are guests. They are chosen, not as VIP's, but as cross-section representative staff members. Miss Benneyan gives them a very practical briefing before they leave—describing proper clothes, travel etiquette, treatment of household employees, if any, and the like.

The UN guests frequently have been able to reciprocate invitations of this sort and thereby further the relationships.

Volunteer Services also arranges outings of various sorts for UN employees, in which private hosts are not involved. At Camp

Nawakwa, near Lake Sebago, New York, for instance, they got typical American summer resort swimming, rowing, hiking, dancing, etc., at a special price of five dollars a person for both housing and meals. And, again, before going they had spade-is-a-spade briefing on manners, clothes and customs, to obviate all possible embarrassment.

There are other amusements available after working hours, closer to home. The *Secretariat News*, like any local American paper, takes note of badminton tournaments, meetings of the Art Club and the Bridge Club, rhythmic gym classes, golf tournaments. There is a section of fifty-six seats in Carnegie Hall available to UN staff members on Sunday afternoons at half-price. For the special pleasure of the distaff side many New York stores give UN discounts. Florida holiday trips have been offered at reduced prices. There is bowling and a stamp club.

Again in the private life area, the UN has a Staff Counselor, Mrs. Dora Kowarski, whose job it is to help not only with the usual difficulties of being an alien, but also with the really personal problems of staff members, the ones that aren't amenable to group treatment.

Money is naturally one of these. The UN Credit Union is useful for the more standard loan purposes, but there are cases of exceptional need it cannot cover. For example, a man with a wife and two children at home collapses from stomach ulcers. He needs extensive medical care and rest. Mrs. Kowarski spends a day working out solutions for the various problems that result in that home. And taps the UN Staff Benevolent Fund to help with expenses.

The first rule of the Staff Counselor's office is that information divulged there stays there. No one outside it has a right to see the records or demand any disclosure of what they contain in connection with individuals. When new Secretariat personnel are briefed, this is one of the things they are told. Otherwise, there is no publicity for the confidential service, no urging that the staff use it. Yet, in three and a half years, fifteen hundred problems were brought for consideration.

A large proportion of these were primarily a matter of blowing off steam. The UN has an employee organization called the Staff Council with representatives in all offices available for consultation or complaint on practically anything and everything that can happen to Headquarters personnel, from rate of pay to prices in the cafeteria. The Council has a joint Appeals Board and an Administrative Tribunal for the more difficult or high-level-policy questions, and the latter has power (which it has been known to use) to set aside decisions of the Secretary-General. Nevertheless, the Staff Counselor spends a great deal of time listening to expressions of discontent over working conditions, salaries and superiors.

Visas for "terminated" employees are a recurring puzzle. Since many countries nowadays have sudden and violent changes of political complexion, sometimes of sovereignty as well, their nationals often do not dare go home after losing UN jobs. On the other hand, they do not have and cannot get credentials from their new governments either to go elsewhere or stay here. In the case of a Chinese, the Staff Counselor's office managed to arrange a displaced person status.

It would be surprising if romance failed to make some sort of appearance in such an office. One instance that called for a search of the statute books is recountable. A field worker in one of the agencies, off in some wild and distant area on UN business, wanted to marry an American girl. But her parents refused to let her join him, or leave the country, before the ceremony was performed. He couldn't return. So the Staff Counselor had to arrange a marriage by proxy. This wasn't quite so easy as had been expected, because not all states permit proxy marriages, but Mrs. Kowarski found one that did, and they lived happily ever afterward.

For emergency medical aid the 3,300 employees have available a well-equipped modern clinic in the Secretariat Building. But, rather typically, one of its main uses is for inoculation of UN travelers against cholera or typhoid or whatever diseases they are likely to encounter on business in far places.

This item of travel is a major characteristic of life in UN-ville. The people here are willing at least, and mostly eager, to go places. Partly it's out of normal human curiosity and venturesomeness. But partly, too, it's because the world rather literally seems to them to be their oyster—or, perhaps more accurately, everybody's oyster. The UN idea is essentially the One World idea, with everyone a citizen. Since it's a citizen's duty as well as his privilege to know his own land, an international civil servant of the UN has a particular call to see the world.

The international civil servant not only has an urge to see the world physically, but also to see it in his mind's eye functioning as it might, smoothly, the parts working in unison instead of clashing and banging and breaking one another to bits. And he has an ability to keep that comprehensive image spread fast on his retina while concentrating patiently on the particular tiny part of the repair work that's his own assignment, just as a watchmaker delicately and painstakingly adjusts the hairspring while considering the ideal operation of the watch as a whole. In less fancy terms this means seeing a happier future for the human race in teaching an Afghanistan farmer how to use a hoe, tenaciously arguing a minor point of parliamentary procedure, saving a dollar on maintenance expense, filing letters or even pounding out a routine press release.

Nothing, of course, is easy—least of all getting along with human beings. But the wider-than-usual outlook on life that evidently goes with UN work seems to have a lubricating effect on human relations. With the exceptions necessary to prove the rule, staff members present to the world a uniformly pleasant front of courtesy and helpfulness. It's conspicuous enough in a country given to rough pleasantries for an observer to wonder if they regard themselves as constantly on exhibition. Perhaps they do.

But if all this dedication and human-kindness concentrated in one community seem a bit overpowering, it should be noted that ordinary human squabbles do occur—and jockeying for position, and envy and various other well-known failings. Perhaps a UN colloquialism will illustrate the general point. High officials are distinguishable by their fine views of the East River, but there are varying degrees of elevation among them and these are marked by the number of office windows. Hence, a "three-pane pasha" is well up in the hierarchy, but a "four-pane pasha" tops him.

UN-ville may not be precisely what town boosters like to call "a big happy family," but it is the only place in history where the whole world has hung its hat and gone to work on the common problems of mankind.

CHAPTER 3

The UN Nobody Knows

THE UN Vishinsky knows in one way and the UN some American tabloid newspapers know in another are puzzlingly different from the UN any nonpartisan citizen can see for himself in New York.

But there is another UN that few Americans know about at all, a UN that may be more important in the long run than the one represented by political talk in the Assembly or Security Council.

This UN, or rather this part of the UN, is unromantically called the Specialized Agencies. A fair bet against any group of Quiz Kids would be to name them.

They are: World Health Organization, Food and Agriculture Organization of the United Nations, United Nations Educational, Scientific and Cultural Organization, International Labour Organisation, International Monetary Fund, International Bank for Reconstruction and Development, Universal Postal Union, World Meteorological Organization, International Telecommunication Union and International Civil Aviation Organization.

Oddly enough, there are three of these Agencies that the Russians continue to support, though they have left the other seven flat.

Let's have a look at all ten of the Specialized Agencies, and at UNICEF (United Nations International Children's Fund).

What the UN Does for Health

"They ought to turn it into a hospital," a bartender mutters, pointing over his shoulder toward the UN plant on the East River in New York.

What he and other Americans with the same prejudice forget or don't know is that it really *is* a hospital—probably the biggest, best and farthest-reaching hospital the world has ever known.

Three diseases are the chief concern of the World Health Organization. These are malaria, tuberculosis and the various venereal afflictions, mainly syphilis. They are the most serious and contagious diseases known to mankind, from the point of view both of mortality and economic disability. Where they are endemic or epidemic, there are not only millions of deaths, there are also great areas of land that farmers do not have the strength to cultivate, industries and handicrafts that languish because workers lack the energy to do a proper job.

Since disease and low productivity are an inseparable pair of afflictions, WHO often works with other Specialized Agencies of the UN to bring aid to underdeveloped areas of the world. DDT spraying cuts down the malaria rate, while the Food and Agriculture Organization (FAO) provides expert tilling advice that healthier men and women can then put to good use. With higher incomes and better nourishment they are able to cope with other problems—to increase their productivity further, to learn new skills, to take thought of political matters, eventually to conduct their own health programs. Children in want get special care from UNICEF, in cooperation with WHO and FAO. And here, too, the health effort has a spiraling effect on family productivity. The less burden children are to parents, the more parents can do for children.

"So what if Indonesians *do* have yaws?" is an all too common, calloused attitude of some Americans. And not a very bright attitude, either, for in the long run what's bad for Indonesians—or Africans or Icelanders—is also bad for us.

It is a significant but frequently ignored fact that disease in our time travels just as fast as the airplane. A plague-bearing flea can attach itself to the clothing of a visitor in a Middle Eastern bazaar on Monday, and on Tuesday or Wednesday start spreading a blackstar message against isolationism in New York or Chicago.

One of WHO's most vital services is in this field. Twenty-four hours a day, every day, WHO monitors stand by the radio and telephone in Geneva, Switzerland, where the Agency's headquarters are located. Once they heard a message from Panama that yellow fever had broken out. At this crossroads of the Western Hemisphere a true epidemic could have been dreadful. But the instantaneous WHO organization of vaccines and medical crews broke the back of the threat in four days.

Another time a ship arrived at Singapore with one crew member suffering from a high temperature and other symptoms of bubonic plague. Radio messages to and from Geneva promptly got the vessel into quarantine, while WHO did electronic detective work. No flea-bearing rats were found at the arrival port, so WHO operatives had to check backward to the source of the ship's cargo. There, deep in the Asian inland, another case of the plague was tracked down and the two were connected by fleas found in the ship's baled rice cargo. The inland breeding place was immediately marked off, and WHO had an unheralded victory over the spread of disease.

By the end of 1952, in two years of operation, WHO had given direct help to more than a hundred governments and territories. WHO's regular expenses in 1952 came to $7,677,000. Under the UN's expanded Technical Assistance Program it was allotted an additional five million for public health projects.

The idea of attacking disease, along with poverty and ignorance, on a concerted world-wide basis, using the best talents of all the world's nations, was so startling and stimulating when it first seemed practicable, under UN auspices, that the disappointment over present-day limitations on financial support is understandable. But a great deal has been accomplished, even in so short a time and with such meager financing.

Take the VD campaign. (Actually, syphilis is the only strictly venereal disease in this operational category. But yaws and bejel, though not transmitted venereally, have similar symptoms and results, and respond to the same treatment. Therefore the mass international attack on them goes along with the attack on syphilis.)

Dr. Brock Chisholm, former head of WHO, spoke of the experiment in VD control his experts conducted among sailors touching at the key port of Rotterdam in Europe. Historically speaking, Rotterdam has been one of the world's prime sources of syphilis— not only because ships carried it from there to the ports of other continents, but also because the sailors of smaller vessels spread it along the Rhine Valley, right through the heart of Europe.

Obviously, the eradication of syphilis among any group as migratory as sailors presents problems. But the WHO experiment has had success. Aside from modernized methods of diagnosis (the quick Kahn and Kline tests) and treatment (penicillin), the important factor in its success was innovation of the treatment book, a document like a passport that each patient carries with him. It shows his entire clinical history of syphilis, together with the dates and other particulars of his treatment up to the moment. On presentation of the book he gets whatever further care is indicated, free, in any port through which he passes.

WHO gives expert technical advice on the treatment of syphilis, supervises conferences of medical people, and even offers fellowships for the training of nurses and doctors in underdeveloped countries (the whole country of Ethiopia, as an example of the need for such training, had only forty-four doctors, with all but two of them practicing in Addis Ababa). The present working aim is less cure than control.

Preliminary WHO surveys showed large areas of Europe and Asia where half the people were syphilitic, some places where the incidence rose to 90 per cent. World War II, in the manner of all wars, brought a great increase of VD, but it also brought the magic drug, penicillin. So WHO decided in favor of a mass attack on syphilis, to match its mass attacks on malaria and tuberculosis. One of the early trial raids occurred in the remote Ghund Valley of India, where 65 per cent of the entire population had positive blood tests.

Every infected person in the valley was given a single shot of penicillin. Five months later check teams returned to assess the results. Their tests turned up no new cases. The single-shot penicillin drive had completely stopped the spread of the disease.

With yaws, bejel and pinta, disfiguring and often incapacitating diseases that plague great areas of the Orient, an injection or two of penicillin does even more. It cures them. A never-ending miracle of satisfaction to UN field workers is to see a crippled youngster, covered with dreadful sores, get his injection and within a few days turn up as sound as a bell.

Yaws, bejel and pinta run a close race to syphilis in causing human misery and economic loss. Some idea of the extent of this economic loss is available in the estimated annual cost of syphilis to United States industry alone: a hundred million dollars—and this doesn't include hospital and medical care—just loss of productivity. An antiyaws campaign in Haiti, involving single penicillin shots, sent 100,000 people back to work and increased Haitian national production by five million dollars a year.

Greece was the scene of intensive antimalaria measures by WHO teams. Food and Agriculture experts got up figures on the economic results. Before DDT spraying, farm families in malarious areas had an average gross income per year of $196.34—starvation to American minds, but well above the world average. After the insecticide campaign, income in those same areas promptly rose to $385.15. And the land healthy farmers found themselves able to cultivate increased by 67 per cent. As incidental benefits, DDT eradication of flies along with the mosquitoes sharply reduced typhoid fever and dysentery; chickens relieved of their pest afflictions laid more eggs; cows gave 15 to 20 per cent more milk. The annual cost of this antimalaria campaign, per person protected, was approximately equivalent to that of a couple of quinine tablets. In the light of the suffering of 300,000,000 victims of malaria the world over (with annual deaths 3,000,000), it seems insignificant.

At the end of World War II millions of children in Europe and Asia were undernourished, underclothed and often homeless— prime targets for tuberculosis. The first winter three million children in eleven European countries got emergency food as a primary measure through UNICEF, then clothing. Afterward, UNICEF and WHO together began the biggest mass vaccination program in history, specifically against tuberculosis, with the preparation called BCG. In Asia alone 9,000,000 children have been tested with tuberculin, 3,200,000 of them vaccinated. The world program calls for testing nearly 60,000,000 children and vaccinating wherever TB has so far failed to penetrate.

The guess is that tuberculosis takes five million lives a year, but it's often a slow killer and, aside from BCG vaccination, the educational and nutritional measures used to fight against it are hard to assess on a readily understandable basis of statistics. Nevertheless, an item from Detroit, Michigan, where there has been a five-year program aimed at control of the disease, gives indication of the benefits that should accrue from WHO's work. The Detroit experiment—not cheap in the spectacular sense of DDT spraying to get rid of malaria—nevertheless saved $1,400,000 a year in sanitaria costs alone. Detroiters spent $200,000 on the program.

WHO has many other purposes besides fighting the diseases mentioned above. Its over-all aim is to advise and help member countries, of whom there are more than seventy, in setting up and operating efficient national health services on their own. A prodigious amount of training is needed in underdeveloped areas. Up to the end of 1952 WHO granted 2,600 fellowships to doctors, nurses and sanitary engineers from seventy countries. It provides consultants for schools; supplies medical literature, laboratory material and teaching equipment; and it has organized a variety of special training centers, seminars and demonstrations in many countries.

WHO's work is divided roughly into three categories: (1) advisory services to governments particularly with regard to control of communicable diseases and training public health workers; (2) central technical services in many fields, such as health statistics, standardizing therapeutic substances, health research; (3) emergency aid in epidemics and disasters.

The communicable diseases against which WHO battles by no means stop with those already mentioned. Its experts have helped in the control of typhus in Afghanistan, plague and cholera in India, leprosy in Ceylon, filariasis (elephantiasis) in South Thailand, cerebrospinal meningitis in the Sudan, trachoma in China and the Philippines, and in various other places worked with less bizarre-sounding maladies like diphtheria, whooping cough, hookworm, smallpox, rabies and poliomyelitis. In both London and Washington it maintains influenza centers for study of this practically universal affliction.

Once some TV people were preparing a program about the UN's Specialized Agencies and a clever one got the idea of showing three maps of the world. The first was to outline illiteracy. On top of that was to go a tracing of the areas of hunger, and, finally, over both the others a tracing of the world geography of ill health. It was a nice idea, but it didn't work out for video—because the three maps were identical in outline and showed up on the screen as only one. The incident, however, has been used often to illustrate dramatically how closely related so many different efforts of the UN turn out to be.

It's hard sometimes to hold people's attention with world-embracing concepts. The figures get too big, the masses of sufferers too great to hold our sympathy as human individuals. But WHO sometimes is able to give help in a humanly dramatic way that we can all understand and appreciate.

A mother from South Africa, visiting in London, became dangerously ill and entered a hospital. The doctors were sure she would die without a blood transfusion. But they knew her blood was a rare variant of Blood Group O that occurs in only one person out of every twenty thousand. Without precisely the same variant of Group O a transfusion would have been as fatal as no transfusion at all.

When news of her plight was broadcast offers of donations came in from Germany, France, Holland and Denmark, as well as from England. Out of 998 blood samples tested one offered by a Somerset blacksmith turned out to be right. The transfusion was flown to London and the woman's life was saved.

Now WHO had nothing to do with the hospital in which this

woman lay, nor with the broadcast of her story. Where it entered
the picture was deep in the background. Under its auspices international standards for blood-grouping had been agreed upon and
named. Thus, the symbol R″ R″ (cdE/cdE), which the South
African mother gave as her blood type, was immediately understandable to the London doctors and they made no mistake in the
transfusion.

It is this work of international standardization that should have
special meaning for ordinary citizens, but rarely receives their
attention. WHO's *International Pharmacopoeia* has standardized the
titles, definitions and standards of identity, quality, strength and
purity of drugs in common use. What this means to the ordinary
citizen is that he can take a prescription to a drugstore with confidence, whether he's in Teheran or home in Topeka.

A committee of WHO does the same job for so-called "biologicals"
—things like insulin, penicillin, vaccines—that are more difficult
to test for uniformity. A diabetic victim can tell you how important
standardization of product is with insulin.

WHO has one other important responsibility of this sort. It is
the question of addiction as applied to drugs. WHO has to decide
whether any new drug is habit-forming or not. Old-time "dope" was
simple enough to identify: opium, morphine, heroin, hashish, co-
caine. But the chemists are busy nowadays with a thousand new
pain-killers and sleeping pills. WHO has to determine what ones
are reasonably safe and what ones to oppose. By agreements among
the member nations its findings have the force of law, in the signatory countries.

One of WHO's important services mentioned earlier but not named
is jaw-breakingly called the Epidemiological Intelligence Service.
This is the Geneva office that keeps a twenty-four-hour-a-day watch
for outbreaks of the plague and other epidemic diseases. If we think
of it at all, we think of it as fast-acting protection against jet-speed
spread of horrible diseases from poverty-stricken foreign lands to
our shores. But the jet-speed spread can work the other way, too
—and has. Although poliomyelitis usually is thought of by experts

as a plague on privileged countries and doctors in underdeveloped countries sometimes have trouble recognizing the symptoms, it not so long ago broke out in India and in Chile, and WHO had to send "iron lungs" after it—by air.

What the UN Does for Food Production

With Americans the only serious problem about food is finding money to buy it. Our farms are hugely productive and could be even more so. The aim here for a long time has been to control our output in such a way that food doesn't glut the markets and depress prices to the point where farmers lose money.

To listen to the acrimonious debate over "parity prices" and watch the heated pulling and hauling that go on in American politics over support or nonsupport of markets for farmers' produce, you might not think of our agricultural situation as happy. If so, you ought to look at the rest of the world.

The problem for agriculturally backward countries—which means a very large part of the world—is the brutal fact that food production falls behind what's needed to keep the population alive. At the same time world population increases at a faster rate than farm produce. Over a fifteen-year period from 1934 to 1949 the respective rates of increase were 9 per cent for food, 12 per cent for people. Therefore, starvation, or at the best hunger, is the common lot of most human beings.

Someone put it this bluntly: "If you killed off half the people in the underdeveloped countries, which contain about two-thirds of the human race, there still wouldn't be enough food for the men, women and children left alive in the world."

It seemed to those who set up the UN Food and Agriculture Organization that a concerted effort to increase food production would be not only more humane than this, but more practical. After all, centuries of disease, semistarvation and two colossal world wars failed to dent rising population totals. In fact, they rose ever more rapidly. It's calculated that an extra mouth to feed appears on earth every one and a half seconds, day in and day out, year in and year out.

Moreover, looking at the results of FAO's 1946 world food survey (the first such survey ever attempted), the experts were convinced the job could be done. A good part of their confidence stemmed from the clear fact that in literate, healthy, energetic countries, where modern methods were used, surplus crops were common and easily could be increased if markets for them existed. Later FAO experiments, usually in combination with other UN Specialized Agencies, such as the World Health Organization, proved some of the practical possibilities in specific areas. But no more than a beginning can be claimed and there are formidable obstacles.

An FAO technical expert named W. W. Dickinson returned from ten months spent on the rich soil of northern Afghanistan and in an interview gave some fascinating examples of these obstacles. He is a cotton expert and was sent abroad under the Technical Assistance Program to advise on how to improve Afghan cotton production.

Dickinson's problems began in the United States, because he could find little or no useful information about the place he was being sent—not even weather reports. Not knowing the weather, he couldn't judge in advance the likeliest type of cotton and had to take with him a variety of seed, choosing it in places along the same parallel of latitude in the United States, from the East to the West Coast.

In the walled capital of Afghanistan, Kabul, most of the government ministers had never made the mountainous trip to the north where he was scheduled to work and had no idea what equipment might be there for his use. Three hundred miles later by jeep Dickinson saw it: some old steel-beam turning plows that he dated to the time of Noah, and some awkward old mattocks that weighed about twelve pounds apiece. When he asked for small common garden hoes the Afghans looked blank. They'd never heard of such things.

Thus, Dickinson's first job in Afghanistan was to design a hoe and have a hundred copies made. Later he had to teach his workers how to use them. They wanted to thin the standing cotton out by hand, but he insisted on at least this much of modern methods, and after a few hours of instruction they were hoeing away as familiarly as if they'd been born on a Mississippi plantation. Still later, when they saw his methods bringing three and a half times the former yield, they got their Government to order thirty thousand hoes.

Dickinson could, he claimed, make it seven times the former yield with fertilizer, but here he ran into different obstacles. Cottonseed cake turned out to be the best available fertilizer, but it was used as fuel in their pottery plants and, aside from grass, weeds and twigs, there was practically nothing else they *could* use in that treeless country. Moreover, there was FAO competition for the cottonseed cake. The sheep expert wanted it for winter feed, and he finally won the battle.

Nevertheless, Dickinson made a strong impression with that three-and-a-half-fold increase. His first year he trained eight agricultural students to spread the gospel of modernization, his second year thirty. These students teach farmers to use the new methods and also other students who will spend their full time teaching other farmers and students so that the lesson spreads quickly.

The Afghan Government sent him back to the United States to buy forty-five tractors, then return and set up a three-thousand-acre model plantation in the north, plus a five-hundred-acre one in the south. Maintenance men have to be shipped in along with the tractors. The Afghan Government also bought fifteen thousand new spindles from Germany, to double the country's weaving capacity, counting on Dickinson's expanded cotton production to feed them. Afghanistan previously had to import all but 10 per cent of its cloth.

Dickinson said that once you gained the Afghans' confidence there was nothing they wouldn't do to follow your suggestions. But he admitted their beginning attitude was "negative," even though they realized they were behind the times and needed to change.

Obviously, diplomacy was as much a requirement of success as technical competence. Asked what co-operation he had to get for his work, he said with telling unadornment: "The provincial governors, the central government, the farmers and the village chiefs." Hardly a soft assignment.

The language difficulty he overcame by acquiring a loyal and intelligent interpreter. But Dickinson "nearly had to break his neck" before he got him to translate accurately. Eastern politeness sometimes prevented him from passing along statements that might be unwelcome, and his employer couldn't be sure he knew what was going on.

Two main points stick out like sore thumbs from Dickinson's report. One is the almost incredible primitiveness of the tools and methods used in backward areas. The other is the farmers' eagerness and ability to adopt new methods—once they've been shown their value. Add a third: that it's neither a quick nor easy job to show them.

When FAO began in 1945 its job wasn't on quite such a grassroots level. It had to gather statistics, as in the world food survey mentioned above, and arrange to have member nations (sixty-six now) pool such information regularly. It set up a Council to keep business going between annual meetings of the governing body, the FAO Conference. One of the Council's duties is to keep a watchful eye on price trends and supplies, and send notice around when surpluses or shortages seem likely to occur, so that interested parties may take proper action.

All this may sound pretty routine, but, as usual in new undertakings, surprises occur. FAO statisticians were gathering the facts about rice—most important single item of life in much of the Oriental world. They were comparing annual production totals of various areas and came upon one area whose figures went something like this: "1947—2,000,000 tons; 1948—2,100,000 tons; 1949—27,-800,000 tons; 1950—2,200,000 tons." The 1949 total was so wildly out of proportion that they rubbed their eyes and asked the government in question for confirmation or explanation. It's not certain they ever got either in satisfactory terms, but they learned something valuable about the workings of civil service minds in that part of the world.

The system of gathering such figures, roughly, was that the leading man of each little village, whatever his title, would estimate the local crop. These local estimates were put together at higher and higher levels of government till they reached the bureau where civil servants, who thought of themselves as having a position worth capitalization, did the final totting up and set the sum down in their books. Their addition was faultless, it was properly entered in the books, and it was no part of their duty to question or criticize if something had gone haywire beneath them, so that was the end of it.

Despite such minor contretemps, FAO managed to compile enormously useful background material. It got together an organization of more than six hundred workers, a large proportion of them food or agricultural scientists, and set up headquarters first in Washington, then, in 1951, in Rome, Italy. The present Director-General is Norris E. Dodd, a farmer from Oregon, who was U.S. Undersecretary of Agriculture before joining the FAO staff.

By 1950, when the UN Expanded Technical Assistance Program got under way, FAO was ready to accept the largest share of its first twenty-million-dollar budget—largest because it was agreed that increased food production and management was the most immediately important project for Technical Assistance. Already FAO had had pertinent experience. For European dairy herds depleted by the war, FAO experts had provided several solutions: the latest techniques of artificial insemination, a vaccine to control contagious abortion, means of curing mastitis. In Greece FAO nutritionists had started a school breakfast feeding plan for children, helped to set up nutrition education programs and to establish a government nutrition service.

In 1949 FAO established a seed fund of outstanding varieties of cereals, grasses, legumes, oilseed crops and vegetables, from which member countries take samples for experimental purposes. FAO gets performance records on the seeds and gives this information to any-one interested.

Earlier, in 1947, knowing the advantages of hybrid corn seed (it produces three-quarters of a billion more bushels of corn in the United States than farmers could grow with the older, open-pol-linated varieties), FAO began sending it to twenty countries of Europe and the Near East, and more recently to India, for experi-mental planting. You probably have seen pictures of some of the results towering over the heads of Iowa visitors. These hybrids can be bred for a variety of characteristics to meet local conditions—to resist pests and diseases, to thrive on drought or excess moisture, to mature early or late, etc. It will take time to test all the possi-bilities for best results in all the varied conditions of the countries to which the sample seeds were sent, but early indications, such as a 25 to 30 per cent yield increase in the Mediterranean area, pointed to success.

Spreading agricultural know-how isn't always a one-way matter. The United States experts have found a few things in their wander-ings that they knew nothing about before—a Japanese-developed sweet potato on Formosa, for example, with a higher starch content and a higher yield. A disease-resistant bell pepper found near Lan-chow in China, and an early-maturing muskmelon in the same area. A frost-resistant apricot in Thailand.

But perhaps such items aren't too interesting to nonfarmer readers. Fish may be more so. FAO knew that the most important need in the diet of undernourished peoples was proteins. Also, that the quickest and easiest way to increase their supply of proteins was with fish.

For technical information on commercial fishing techniques, refrigerating, stocking in ponds, etc., FAO has sent its experts pretty much all around the world. It has sponsored Fisheries Councils in the Indo-Pacific area and in the Mediterranean, offered advice on research, administration and marketing problems. And one of its experts, John Fridthjof, even organized a widely publicized promo-tion stunt in Santiago, Chile.

Not to be misunderstood, he called it Fish Week. Publicizing it with thousands of posters and pamphlets, daily radio talks, lectures at the University of Chile and recipe give-aways, he drew 250,000 visitors to his displays on Santa Lucia hill, above the city of Santiago. Here he had a small museum showing fishery development in the country, and a movie theater that gave evening performances of fishery subjects made in Canada, the United Kingdom and the Scandinavian countries. Commercial booths on the hill sold 35,000 kilos of fried hake during the week. And at the end of the week the Chilean Minister of Economy and Trade announced that the following year (1952) his Government would spend $3,720,000 on new shore facilities for fishing activities and on modernizing fishing craft and gear. Fish Week thus turned out to be both a business and an FAO triumph.

More than 90 per cent of the world's fish food has been taken from the waters of the Northern Hemisphere, usually in the shallow depths off the edges of continents. No one knows how far mankind really could go in exploitation of this ready-and-waiting source of nutrition, particularly the deep-sea variety. But FAO is doing a good deal of work on the subject of fresh water specimens that may be more meaningful to low-income inlanders who can't pay the cost of transportation and refrigeration from the seas.

There is a pleasant story about fresh water fish and the FAO. It starts back in 1939, before either the FAO or the UN was born, when a fish culture expert named W. H. Schuster was visiting an Indonesian fish farmer. The farmer displayed five fingerlings he'd raised in his pond and while Mr. Schuster looked curiously at them one released spawn from its mouth, then another did the same. They were mouth-breeders. Furthermore, they were mouth-breeders of an African species called *Tilapia*, native to the coast of Mozambique and never before seen either in Indonesia or any of the thousands of miles of water between Indonesia and Mozambique. How they made the trip no one is likely ever to know.

But Mr. Schuster instantly saw a practical point that overshadowed the mystery. Since fresh water fish usually spawn only in rivers or special breeding ponds, fish farms have to be restocked each season with fingerlings caught in streams—no easy task—or raised in hatcheries. But the *Tilapia* bred without a tremor in fresh, stagnant, brackish or salt water. They were just what the fish culture expert ordered for Indonesia.

The *Tilapia's* young were introduced into other Indonesian ponds and by the time Mr. Schuster got back from his war years in Japanese prison camps they had increased and multiplied to the status of a staple food. The Japanese propaganda experts found it worth while to claim their country had introduced the fish.

In 1950 FAO sent a couple of hundred *Tilapia* from Indonesia to Thailand, where they bred as happily as in Indonesia, and by the end of 1952 numbered 100,000. In the markets of Bangkok the Thais are glad to pay as much for them as they do for the most popular native fish.

Mr. Schuster's fingerlings clearly are making a peaceful conquest of Asia.

It comes as a minor shock to some people to learn that trees are as much a responsibility of the Food and Agriculture Organization— even when they don't bear fruit—as hake or cotton plants or cattle. But the reasons, when stated, are clear enough.

Wood is used for cooking (though coal and gas and electricity are, too). Timber is raw material for construction, for plastics, for paper, for textile fibers. Farmers use trees as windbreaks and they need the forests to check soil erosion and to help keep water from flowing away to the sea too fast. Trees and forests need scientific care and protection to grow, and they need other kinds of attention to prevent their waste and to encourage their replacement.

World War II destroyed a tragic number of homes in Europe that could have been most easily and quickly replaced with wooden structures. But artillery and aerial bombing also destroyed forests. Lack of wood presented itself at the end of the war as one of the toughest obstacles to restoring housing for the people of all countries involved in the struggle.

FAO studied the problem on a European regional rather than

national basis and made suggestions which resulted in sending to
countries that were still able to export timber millions of dollars'
worth of forestry equipment. By the end of 1948 lumber supplies
had risen almost high enough to meet the demand. The UN Economic Commission for Europe had a considerable hand in this good
work, but FAO gave most of the technical advice—and influenced
national governments not only to begin large-scale planting of new
forests, but to mesh their forestry programs with those of other
countries into a regional pattern.

The rape of America's unparalleled forests is still an unforgivable
sin, but belated conservation efforts during the past generation have
begun to prove the arguments of their proponents.

Meanwhile, FAO experts study ways to lessen the drain on
Canadian, Swedish and American forests made by the insatiable
hunger for newsprint and the other products of wood pulp, such as
plastics, motor fuel, etc. Late in 1952 a conference of thirty pulp and
paper experts at an FAO conference in Rome concluded that it
would be feasible to establish a brand-new pulp industry based on
tropical and subtropical woods, and also on various leftovers of
tropical agricultural products—sugar-cane bagasse, for example.
They agreed that well-established methods could pulp tropical hard-
woods, as well as lesser woods, and that varying cost factors in less
developed countries (higher chemical, transportation and interest
charges as against lower labor and raw material prices) might balance out and permit actual competition with the old established
pulp industries, in Scandinavia and North America.

Director-General Dodd noted with what seemed like some surprise and a good deal of satisfaction that representatives of private
industry at this conference made no effort to withhold their knowledge and experience from the FAO members, but worked right
along with everyone else toward getting the facts as straight as
possible.

You have a good chance, then, in the not too distant future, of
reading a morning newspaper that stems from a Borneo bamboo

forest, while your wife brings in breakfast wearing a plastic apron that started life as Philippine teak.

For different reasons many areas of the world have been denuded of forests, some almost entirely of trees. The obvious advantages of soil and water conservation afforded by woodlands make these lands a subject of interest to FAO. Since the only continent in the world without a eucalyptus is Antarctica, since it is a tree that proverbially grows fast and has almost as many uses as species, which number a thousand, FAO forestry experts focused their attention for reforestation purposes on the eucalyptus. Late in 1952 a group of experts from interested countries went with FAO officials for a two-months tour of Australia, the tree's best-known habitat, to learn all they could of its foibles, care and usefulness. It seems likely, as a future result, that many improbable places on the globe will have a look of Down Under.

FAO foresters would like to see the best possible use made of existing timber, which partly means reduction of waste; they would like to see definite programs established to maintain the forests that exist, which partly means replanting after cutting; and they would like to create new forests.

One of their troubles in maintaining existing forests required enlisting emergency aid from another FAO branch of experts, the entomologists. Cause of it all was an insect that Americans regard quite properly as a pest but innocuous—the fall webworm (*Hyphantria cunea*) or tent caterpillar. In its native North America the fall webworm is restrained by the lethal discipline of forty different parasites that feed on it. Hence its harmlessness.

But somehow, back in 1940, specimens crossed the Atlantic undetected and passed nervous borders without authority to a place near Budapest in Hungary, where they were first noted. Since then their numberless progeny have infested large areas of Yugoslavia and spread well into Austria. Other Eastern bloc countries besides Hungary are no doubt affected, and nations to the west of Austria are seriously alarmed about *their* prospects.

The hungry larvae of the tent caterpillar, so inoffensive in America, ate every leaf from over a hundred species of temperate zone trees, shrubs and plants, once they got to Europe. The forty types of parasite policemen were left behind in America and the larvae have been wanton in unimpeded destruction of plants and trees.

As an emergency measure the FAO and various European countries had to institute a major spraying and dusting campaign, involving 9,000,000 trees in Yugoslavia, 300,000 in Austria—and not a little money. As a long-term measure FAO sponsored a co-operative research program on the biology of the fall webworm and also the American parasites that have to be exported to do police duty abroad.

FAO has plenty of other problems of a border patrol nature— desert locust control, for example, or helping to establish standards under which plant life may pass from country to country (the Dutch once had to make out eighty different forms for exporting tulip bulbs to different countries; under a new convention sponsored by FAO a single form does for all). There is a possibly apocryphal claim that one ingenious FAO expert invented a machine to halt insect immigration—a kind of large megaphone, with a grinding mechanism at the small end and a sound-maker that imitated the mating call of the male insect. Females flew lovingly in and were ground to bits.

But the key purpose of FAO remains the dissemination of modern scientific knowledge. It has held many scientific meetings, set up training schools and established fellowships (perhaps five hundred of them by the end of 1952) for special training of qualified local people from all over the world.

Perhaps its most dramatic educational effort has been at Pátzcuaro, where FAO, UNESCO and the Mexican Government have joined forces to see what could be done to improve the lives of all the inhabitants of a backward community, in living standards, health and culture, using local resources. The final outcome is by no means yet assessable, but interest has been intense and the full story, when it is ready to be told, should be fascinating.

A practical insurance project FAO hopes one day to set up, but hasn't so far been able to get beyond the discussion stage, is establishment of an Emergency Food Reserve, for ready use in case of disaster anywhere in the world. The scheme has many complications, but it also has many attractions and someday may be a fact.

What the UN Does for the Children

There is a convent on the border between Jewish and Arab territories in the Middle East, where the strife of recent years has uprooted so many families and cost so many lives. UNICEF (the United Nations International Children's Fund) has sent food to the convent since 1948. Not long ago thirty of the inmates decided to show their gratitude. They were five-year-old orphan girls.

With pieces of cardboard, bits of colored stone and odd strips of satin, they put together and lovingly dressed a ten-inch-high figurine. They placed the little statue, shimmering, on an altar in the kindergarten, where all the orphans could see and each remember to give thanks in her own way to the now embodied benefactress they called "Mademoiselle UNICEF."

It seems a shame to many people that an organization so universally admired and loved should have had to lead a hand-to-mouth existence. But that's the case. It was established in December of 1946 by the UN General Assembly, not with the permanent and more or less autonomous character of a regular Specialized Agency, but for a three-year period. Contributions for its support were purely voluntary, by governments and individuals. In December of 1950 the Assembly voted a new three-year lease of life with a view, as UNICEF publications put it, "to establishing the Fund on a permanent basis at the end of that time."

But, although more than half of the world's 900,000,000 children under fifteen are in what amounts to a constant state of need—a state that holds little hope of major improvement for at least a generation—UNICEF, their only practical source of help on a world-wide basis, by mid-1953 seemed to have a future even more uncertain than its past. And the chief cause of uncertainty was the United States.

To most American parents, children present three common problems. One is getting them to eat properly—to balance the dessert with spinach. Another is getting them to dress properly—rubbers in the rain, mufflers in cold weather. The third is getting them to the doctor or the dentist on schedule.

To most parents everywhere else on earth the problems are so different that Americans sometimes have trouble comprehending them. For something like half a billion children there never have been shoes or milk or doctors. And their parents had no choice in the matter.

UNICEF started, in 1946, as a direly needed emergency agency to do something for the thirty million European children whom World War II had made homeless, ragged and starving. Food was the first need and on the advice of the Food and Agriculture Organization, UNICEF supplied it in the cheapest, easiest, most nutritious form—dried skim milk. The first winter three million youngsters in the eleven hardest-hit European countries got this help.

After food came clothing, and UNICEF found the raw materials —cotton, wool and leather, chiefly—from which the needy countries themselves fabricated shoes and shirts, dresses, coats and suits.

Then came the pressing demands of health. With so much malnutrition, lack of proper clothing and destruction of housing, tuberculosis was reaching epidemic proportions. The Scandinavian countries, on their own, made a start to fight it. Then UNICEF stepped in and, with the aid of the World Health Organization, began the historic campaign of vaccination with BCG (initials of the word "bacillus" and the names of the two French scientists who developed the vaccine, Calmette and Guerin). This campaign, when completed on a world-wide basis, will have reached sixty million children tested for tuberculosis with tuberculin and from twenty to thirty million vaccinated. It costs about a dollar to vaccinate twenty-four children. The estimate is that BCG provides about two years of immunity for four-fifths of the children not already infected.

Yaws and malaria and syphilis are diseases of children as well as adults and UNICEF began working with the World Health Organization to fight them on a mass scale. A UNICEF field worker gives a human idea of the results.

One day he saw a fourteen-year-old girl in a UNICEF-WHO clinic on the island of Java, where yaws has been a blight for centuries, afflicting four-fifths of the rural population. Despite the fact that one shot of penicillin is usually enough to stop the disease and two shots are almost a sure cure, many Javanese have become fatalistic about it and if they go at all to the clinics do so without much hope.

The field worker says this fourteen-year-old was the most beautiful girl he'd ever seen, with dark, expressive eyes, fine features, a gold-bronze skin. But when he asked, "Aren't you glad you're going to be cured?" she merely shrugged her shoulders. Then he saw how carelessly she was dressed, how little regard she had for her appearance—not even the typical Javanese flower in her hair.

On her way out, an hour or so later, he saw her again. She had talked with other patients, received her injection and there was a new light in her eyes. On a table near the door lay a crimson hibiscus and she stopped to put it in her hair.

The UNICEF worker thought: "I wonder if the lucky young man who gets her will ever know how much he owes UNICEF."

In money, ridiculously little, since one penicillin treatment costs about fifty cents. But in health and hope and happiness something incalculable.

By 1952 two million children in Asia had been tested under UNICEF auspices for yaws, 375,000 treated. The spread of syphilis and bejel, of course, comes under the same program. Twenty million have had protection against malaria, chiefly by DDT spraying, not only in Asia, but also in Central America. And there is the great antituberculosis program.

In the beginning a "cup of milk" was the symbol of UNICEF. At one time there were seven million children "sitting around the UNICEF food table." As economic conditions improved over much of the world, that figure was cut by half, and of the three and a half million still being fed, only 575,000 got their skim milk for the chief purpose of preventing starvation. They were refugee children and those living in drought-stricken areas.

The rest of the three and a half million typified a change in aim for UNICEF. The aim became health for the children, rather than simple survival. In Africa, for example, 340,000 youngsters were fed skim milk to combat a widespread diet deficiency disease called kwashiorkor. In Central America UNICEF joins other UN Specialized Agencies in distributing the skim milk for demonstrations to show its value in improving general child health. Here the idea is to encourage locally mantained school-feeding programs. Similarly, elsewhere in Latin America, in the Eastern Mediterranean and in Asia, maternal and child welfare centers receive the milk.

To offset rickets, as one specific target, and round out children's diets generally, UNICEF also provides fish-liver oil in various forms —our traditional cod liver oil is one. This, again, is in considerable part an educational measure and wherever possible is done through schools. There is a nice story about it from the Philippines.

A thirteen-year-old boy in one of the provinces was night-blind— could see practically nothing after dark. One night he failed to arrive home before sunset. His frantic parents gathered the neighbors and sent searching parties through the jungle. While they were beating the woods, the mother heard someone approaching the house. At first her hopes rose, then she realized it couldn't be her José because of the firm, rapid step. *He* would have been stumbling and bumping into trees. But it was!

"Mama!" José shouted. "I can see!"

And the story came out. José, playing baseball, had forgotten to start home in time and hurried along in fear as the sun went down. It went all the way down long before he reached the nipa hut that was his home, but somehow it never got too dark for him to see. Gradually he realized that his night-blindness was gone and his fear changed to joy.

At school for the month past José had been getting shark-liver capsules from UNICEF. They contain large quantities of Vitamin A, lack of which causes night-blindness.

The whole village was educated that one night.

Much of UNICEF's educational work is carried on in conjunction with the Food and Agriculture Organization. The idea first is to show the value of milk and fish oil to children's health, then to show local populations how to produce their own. In the latter field, the Food and Agriculture Organization naturally has greater competence. It not only demonstrates how to produce more, but also how to use what is produced in the most effective way. In the case of milk this has much to do with pasteurization, refrigeration and drying. UNICEF, up to the middle of 1952, had given equipment for these processes to fourteen countries in Europe, the Middle East and Latin America that now guarantees safe, low-cost or free milk to four million children.

Although UNICEF is not officially a Specialized Agency, its techniques and procedures follow the pattern of other UN organizations. The aim, as with the Food and Agriculture Organization, World Health Organization and others, is first to demonstrate the value of modern methods, then to train native technicians how to apply them and also teach other native technicians. Otherwise, UNICEF has as its main functions to furnish a "nucleus of knowledge and initiative." It gathers the best up-to-date technical knowledge and takes the lead in spreading it. Also, it has a mobile corps of experts ready to send to trouble spots.

In another way UNICEF follows the procedure of such agencies as Food and Agriculture and World Health. It insists that the money it spends in any country be matched by equivalent sums in local effort. That this rule has been carried out is evident from a couple of figures. Up to July 1, 1952, UNICEF's total receipts from governments and individuals (there have, of course, been many voluntary contributions from other-than-governmental sources) were $165,-000,000. The sixty-four countries it had aided spent within their own boundaries the considerably larger sum of $190,000,000, and this was their own money. Beyond that, in gratitude a number of these assisted countries themselves became contributors to the Children's Fund.

On the principle observed elsewhere in the UN, that countries should give support in proportion to their means, the United States always has been the largest dollar contributor to UNICEF. Despite our usual pride in American generosity for such worthy causes, there has been resistance against appropriations for UNICEF and in May, 1953, when sixteen nations voted to continue the children's organization, the United States delegate was the only one to abstain. Even Soviet Russia voted in favor.

If the abstention, implying doubt about continued American support, stemmed back to resentment against the dollar amounts we had previously contributed as compared with those other nations gave, one fact deserves note. On a comparative population, or per capita, basis, the most generous giver was not the United States, but little Iceland. And there were several other countries, on the same basis, that topped our record.

Early in the "cup of milk" program, when the European need for food was worst, someone asked an Italian child what UNICEF meant. He answered: "It's the American word for 'cow.'"

A little later, when UNICEF's aims expanded and supplies began to be sent all over the globe, there was a feeling that the organization's name on crates and boxes ought to be translated into the various languages of receiving countries, or at least the initials forming it into the different alphabets, so that they would be surely recognized. But the packing cases already shipped all bore a standard UNICEF symbol and before a decision was made, "UNICEF" had become an actual word in far parts of Asia, South America, even along the Arctic Circle.

To poverty-stricken parents in scores of now friendly countries the disappearance of that symbol—and the supplies and technicians that bear it—would be a bewildering deprivation for their children.

What the UN Does for Education

Newspaper headlines of the last few years offer a kind of reverse for this heading, something like: "What Some U.S. School Boards Want to Do to the UN." The answer is pretty close to mayhem.

UNESCO (United Nations Educational, Scientific and Cultural Organization) is the chief target of the school boards' enmity, but their dislike often includes the rest of the international organization. In California and Texas, chiefly, though elsewhere, too, it has been freely charged that UNESCO tries to undermine the traditional patriotism of our school children by giving them an ideal of world government. The imputation is that Communists invented the ideal of world government, along with the electric light, airplane, radio and other ideas.

The more practical charge is that UNESCO tries to take control of the American system of education. In several instances UNESCO literature about the UN was cited as an example of the propaganda method in this effort, and, despite argument from substantial sections of the communities involved, teaching about the UN was removed from the schools.

In Los Angeles, which perhaps fought the issue out most bitterly, it happens that the start of the debate came over a little book called *The "E" in UNESCO*. It was signed by Superintendent of Schools Alexander Stoddard, along with the rest of the school board, and issued as Publication No. 498 of the Curriculum Division of Los Angeles City School Districts. None of the signers could very well have been on the payroll of UNESCO.

The closest the book itself came to a philosophy of world government (as anyone who bothers to examine it will see) was to urge international understanding and co-operation. True, these are aims of UNESCO, as they are of the UN as a whole. But they are also explicitly stated objectives of the United States Government, now and for many years past, whether Republican or Democratic. Nevertheless, teaching about the UN was banned in Los Angeles schools, even though in this case it was begun by the school board itself.

It is true that UNESCO makes pamphlets and other teaching materials available to schools that want them. To the observer who tries to be objective, these materials do not seem to have Marxist leanings; they merely try to explain the workings of the UN.

But all this obscures what is probably the main point of UNESCO —a point which one would expect to appeal to practically all Americans. UNESCO's biggest project is to build a kind of "little red schoolhouse" big enough to teach reading and writing and arithmetic to the more than half of all the people in the world who are illiterate. Plus a few other essential forms of knowledge. It's hard for most Americans to realize that there are a billion and a half people on earth who can't read a street sign in any language, tell what merchandise they're buying from the label or write a two-line note. These people can't tot up figures, except in their heads (if they have any idea of figures). They have little or no notion of sanitation, proper nutrition or anything else about domestic science, and practice agriculture about as it was practiced five thousand years ago. It isn't stupidity that makes them so; it's plain ignorance.

UNESCO's strength is being channeled into a gigantic drive to help these people. As an example of the difficulties it faces, there is one small underdeveloped area in Africa where five hundred different dialects are spoken—and less than ten of those five hundred ever have been put into writing by anyone. UNESCO's task in this area would be to decide, first, whether or not to try to reduce the five hundred different dialects into some common writing form, into which the hundreds of dialects all would fit; then work out a way of registering the phonetic sounds of the varying dialects in that common writing form; then teach the value of writing and reading in that form; then teach the natives this brand-new, utterly unthought-of technique; and, finally, prepare some of the better native students to teach the rest of their fellows how to use it.

This is a task that has no real comparison with the American "little red schoolhouse." Here we had a written language many centuries old and a traditional respect for dealing with it on paper. In the jungles and on remote mountain plateaus there is no such background. Scholars have to start from scratch, tuning their ears for strange primitive vocal sounds, translating them into marks on paper, teaching the natives what the marks mean, and, finally, teaching native trainers how to teach their fellow natives what they mean and how to make them, so that knowledge will spread.

A few years ago, India, with its ancient and respected civilization, won independence and set up a democratic form of government. It might have shocked most Americans to know that 85 per cent of the population qualified to vote in the first election could not and did not cast ballots, simply because they couldn't read them. Since they couldn't read newspapers or magazines either, and there were few radios, the names on the ballots and what they represented would have meant little to them anyhow.

An army marches on its stomach. A democracy marches on its ability to read a newspaper. UNESCO proposes to produce this ability in the more than half of the human race that does not have it now. This, UNESCO and the UN consider, is a first step toward universal democracy and away from tyranny.

If you worked the problem out in an ordinary American classroom context, with thirty pupils to a class, and an average of three thousand dollars a year to the teachers, the project would require fifty million instructors and cost one and a half billion dollars a year. The money, of course, is little compared with what we spend on armament, but where would UNESCO find the fifty million teachers?

Actually, UNESCO in 1953 had about $9,350,000 to spend on all its activities. Hence, its only way of spreading "fundamental education" is the same as that of so many other UN Specialized Agencies—"training trainers."

The slogan, "Each One Teach One," which now permeates practically all Specialized Agency Technical Assistance activities, was conceived by an incredibly energetic and purposeful Protestant missionary named Dr. Frank C. Laubach.*

Long before the UN had genesis in Franklin D. Roosevelt's mind, Dr. Laubach back in 1929 began an indomitable, singlehanded attack on world illiteracy. The calculation is that his individual efforts, directly or indirectly, have taught ABC's to some fifteen million persons. He has worked in sixty-four countries and, in his phrase,

* For an excellent full account of his work see the Profile by Robert Rice in *The New Yorker*, February 16, 1952.

"made lessons" in 239 languages or dialects, practically none of which he can speak himself. He has been a valuable adviser to UNESCO, which uses much of his pictorial methodology and counts heavily on his "Each One Teach One" philosophy.

Dr. Laubach started with the savage Moros on the biggest Philippine island, Mindanao. Their only literate citizens wrote and read in Arabic, but the people's language was Maranaw, a fortunately simple language that never before had been put on paper. Dr. Laubach put it on paper for the first time, not so much with the idea of starting a pedagogical revolution as with the purpose of forwarding his evangelical mission, which was financed by the Union Congregational Church of Upper Montclair, New Jersey.

When Dr. Laubach began his fight against illiteracy about 4 per cent of the population in his Lanao province of Mindanao could read and write, in Arabic. Two years later 20 per cent of the population could read and write their native Maranaw in the far simpler Roman alphabet, which he used in "making lessons." And the literacy rate was rising 1 per cent per month. Part of Dr. Laubach's enormous success on Mindanao had a debt to one early pupil who was impressed by the "Each One Teach One" slogan. What this particular Moro savage had to say was: "Everybody who learns has got to teach. If he doesn't, I'll kill him." The disciples knew very well he meant it, and they went out and taught.

But the Moro's approach was miles away from Dr. Laubach's. He is a great unbeliever in "No." He states categorically that no teacher should ever ask a question that the student cannot answer. He believes strongly in the virtues of slapping on the shoulder, smiling at the pupil and saying, in effect: "You're doing fine." None of his lessons lasts a moment longer than the student's attention, and if that fails, he feels it's the lesson's fault, not the pupil's.

On Mindanao Dr. Laubach selected three words that had all the consonant sounds in the language. He wrote each of the words across the top of a large chart, then broke it down below into syllables, giving, along with the syllables as they actually appeared in the word, all possible vowel variants to go with the consonants.

Within an hour or less—sometimes as little as twenty minutes—the student was startled to discover that he had already learned how to read.

In this first venture he was fortunate in having a very simple language to deal with and in being able to deal with it in his own alphabet, since no other existed to interfere. Later projects presented much more serious difficulty and Dr. Laubach had to elaborate his method and suit it to special circumstances in the various countries. The chief addition is pictures, which are adroitly worked out to illustrate language sounds with representations of things whose spoken names coincide with the names of the written character. For example, in Burmese the written character for the sound "wa" is a circle; Dr. Laubach illustrated it with a picture of a very fat boy whose stomach was perfectly round, "wa" being the Burmese word for "fat."

UNESCO experts have added a great deal to Dr. Laubach's system and the "fundamental education" program includes basic teaching in sanitation and domestic science as well as reading and writing. But the missionary's work on Mindanao was valiant pioneering that proved spectacularly how much could be done by a single devoted man. It was something else, too—dramatic proof of the value of such effort.

For three hundred years under Spanish rule of the Philippines the Moros had been intractable thorns in the side of authority. They were never conquered and over the centuries they developed a proud pugnacity that carried on over into the era of American sovereignty. White men went armed on Mindanao as late as 1928, thirty years after the Spanish-American War, and with reason. But within five years of the 1929 start of Laubach's campaign, the Moros changed to peaceful ways and it was possible for Americans to live on the island in safety. The Moros also became sympathetic to Christianity and Dr. Laubach got all the converts he could handle—which was his aim in the beginning.

But, despite that astonishing figure of fifteen million taught to read and write through his efforts, the missionary has remained unhappy about the problem of illiteracy. The annual world population increase in backward areas far outstrips the gains in readers and writers for which he has been responsible. Poor people reproduce more often than those in better circumstances, and ignorance remains as firm a friend of poverty as disease. Only the sort of combined attack on all three that agencies of the UN like UNESCO, the Food and Agriculture Organization, the International Labour Organisation and the World Health Organization have planned and set in operation has any chance of long-term success.

Fundamental education centers, encouraged and advised by UNESCO experts, beginning with the first pilot project in Haiti, now are working in many scattered areas of the world. Perhaps the most interesting is in the Pátzcuaro Lake region of Mexico. UNESCO's Director-General from 1948 to 1952, Jaime Torres Bodet, in the early 1940's was Minister of Education in Mexico and started his own program of fundamental education which in the course of two years, with the familiar "Each One Teach One" slogan, taught 1,200,000 Mexicans how to read and write. For the estimated 70,-000,000 people living in Central and South America who lack these abilities, the Pátzcuaro experiment now offers much wider hope.

It is a joint operation of the Mexican Government, UNESCO and the Organization of American States. In addition, the Food and Agriculture Organization, the World Health Organization and the International Labour Organisation have sent experts. The stated purpose is to raise living standards using only the economic and cultural resources locally available, except for the advice and encouragement of UN and government experts. It is also a kind of UNESCO showcase for fundamental education.

Food and Agriculture field men engage in such homely projects as demonstrating how to prune fruit trees properly, how to control insects in the orchards, how to build a model pig pen, how to drive a tractor. Under their direction the village of Cucuchuco became famous as the first community in the region to install its own practical water system. The Food and Agriculture experts' function is to demonstrate modern ideas in home economics, nutrition and agriculture, to rouse interest in co-operative effort for improvement by the communities, and to train teachers among the natives to spread the new techniques by down-to-earth work in the fields and villages.

One of the biggest problems, as in most underdeveloped areas, is to generate confidence that new ways of cultivating land and caring for livestock are really worth the effort of applying. The trainees who go out to spread this confidence among the people have had remarkable success, largely by practical personal demonstration of what to do and how it succeeds. But there are visual teaching materials, too, provided by the UN agency. Simple though these are, knowledge of reading and writing helps. This, partly, is where UNESCO comes in. Along with teaching handicrafts and teaching students how to make teaching materials.

Half the fourteen thousand inhabitants of the twenty villages in the area were illiterate and not much interested in changing. The pictorial approach helped. Posters were especially useful, but all the known reproducing processes cost too much or presented too great technical difficulties at Pátzcuaro. So, two UNESCO men, Uruguayan Julio Castro and American Jerome Oberwager, decided to work out something new. And they did.

After much experimentation they arrived at what they called the glueplate process—so cheap and so simple that any teacher-artist combination can use it, any carpenter can build the press for running off copies. What they did was to cover a glass plate with a fifty-fifty mixture of paraffin wax and beeswax on which the artist could draw his picture and do his lettering direct, correcting as he went. Then, after lines were cut out with a simple engraving tool, a mixture of glue and glycerine was poured over the wax, allowed to solidify and removed, thus providing the stereotype or printing surface. They inked it, smoothed paper over it (any size can be used) and had a fine reproduction. The cost—less than two cents.

UN field workers have to be ingenious and ready to meet local needs everywhere. At Pátzcuaro, however, they perform on a kind of dual stage. Not only do they extemporize to raise the standard of living for the Indians of the immediate region, but also furnish an instructive drama for visiting teams of trainees from at least seventeen other Latin-American countries. These visiting teams go about the Pátzcuaro area with the local trainees, watching them at their work of teaching others. Then they go home to their own countries and each one starts teaching one in an ever widening circle. As it widens, the seventy million Latin Americans who cannot read and write will have an ever increasing chance to learn.

But fundamental education is by no means the only important function of UNESCO. On a higher intellectual level (for those who benefit), it serves as an exchange bureau for scientific and cultural information of every conceivable sort. It helps libraries to collect books. It has catalogued both in French and English the fine collection of recorded folk music from all over the world in the French National Record Library in Paris. It sponsored an international treaty that went into effect early in 1952 abolishing import duties on a wide range of educational, scientific and cultural materials. It helped to set up an educational film center in Turkey. It sponsored a meeting in Brooklyn, New York, of forty-five museum experts and educators from twenty-five countries in Europe, Asia and the Americas, in part to promote the international establishment of mobile museum units, international exchanges of staff and the creation of more fellowships. It has set up the system of UNESCO Gift Coupons, which are a form of international currency that facilitates the purchase of books and other cultural materials. It persuaded the Universal Postal Convention to lower postal rates on newspapers and periodicals.

Now and then UNESCO sponsors a special project to which people with long-standing special opinions may object. One such project was publicized in *Life* Magazine, May 18, 1953. It was a three-year study by sociologists, anthropologists and geneticists from all over the world on the controversial subject *What Is Race?* The major conclusions of the scientists were that the three main races of the world—Caucasian, Negroid and Mongoloid—show little or no variation in intelligence and aptitude, though they do have genetic differences that make for the differences in their outward appearance, and that, as the races mingle more freely, as they are doing, even the genetic differences may disappear.

What the UN Does for Labor

"We took the initiative and we are not going to be thrust aside so easily as all that. I have written to Lloyd George to tell him so. I'm not going to let him do this to me."

This was Albert Thomas speaking as first Director of the International Labour Office of the League of Nations, in 1920. It doesn't sound so heretical today, perhaps, but at the time Lloyd George was key member of the League's Supreme Council, and the Supreme Council, which had just dictated the terms of peace after World War I, held such a remote, lofty and powerful place in the scheme of things that hardly anyone thought of publicly disagreeing with its policy decisions, let alone writing Mr. Lloyd George a direct letter of dissent. Particularly a dissent that said his august tribunal was usurping the privilege of a small and not much regarded offshoot of the League.

It really was heresy at the time and other members of ILO, who had not yet come to know Albert Thomas well, almost literally shook in their boots.

His difference with Lloyd George, pertinently enough for us today, had to do with Soviet Russia. ILO had suggested what would be known now as an investigating committee to go see what actually was happening in the new Soviet State. The suggestion won a good deal of public attention, since people were hardly less curious then than they are now about the Russian situation, and the Supreme Council took note. But their way of taking note was to consider a Commission of Enquiry of their own, not of ILO. It was to this that Albert Thomas objected.

In the end no League of Nations or ILO inquirers made the junket, but Director Thomas' letter to Lloyd George had the unusual effect of bringing ILO up for discussion during an entire Supreme

Council meeting. The Labour Office never before had had such prominence.

But it has had prominence ever since.

Among the UN Specialized Agencies ILO holds the unique position of being the only organization that bridges the gap between the old League of Nations and the present UN. The International Telecommunication Union and the Universal Postal Union are considerably older in years than ILO, but they were not connected with the League. They did their necessary business independently.

ILO started as a kind of stepchild of the League, not exactly unwanted but hopefully understood to be in the background. An idea of the situation may be had from one incident. ILO headquarters were temporarily in London. For expenses the treasurer of ILO gave a check made out for him personally to an English member of the staff, who was to set up an office account. The £5,000 check was on the Bank of England. When the ILO staff member took it to his own bank the manager first asked: "What is the International Labour Office?" Then, after a full explanation, he continued to look doubtful, suggesting that a resolution of the ILO Governing Body (which was not due to meet for another six weeks) would really be necessary before accepting such an account. And finally insisted that the ILO staff member deposit the check in his own account (which had rarely held more than £4), if he must have immediate action, adding dolefully: "Do you realize that if you were run over and killed when you leave the bank the money will be the legal property of your heirs?" As the staff member later wrote:

For six months the whole of the funds of the International Labour Office remained at the mercy of the traffic in London and Genoa until, when the Office at last reached Geneva, proper and regular arrangements were made. It should be added, as a further indication of our financial difficulties, that there were times when, had a fatal accident occurred, any dispute between unscrupulous heirs and the Office would have been over something less than a five pound note.

There was something else that E. J. Phelan (who was the ILO staff member just quoted, and who wrote an excellent biography of

Albert Thomas) described in considerable humorous detail. Again, it may not sound like a great deal for today, but it was important. Since the United States would have nothing to do with President Wilson's creation, Great Britain and France naturally took leading parts in the League. Since neither had ever tried such an undertaking with the other before, and since both had rather violently differing concepts of government administration—and of the civil servant's function at varying levels of authority—there was probably bound to be misunderstanding and friction. In this case the conflict of ideas came to a hilarious head over a public relations man's "in" and "out" basket and the British Civil Service Registry system, which kept documents in a central file till called for or unless they were routed on to someone else in the organization. The system called for initialing the slip on a routed paper or document once the interested person had finished with it. But this the press relations man hadn't learned. And, since it was part of his job to see practically everything that went through the office, he had a certain justification for hysteria. The mountains of papers he waded through one day and put in his "out" basket kept returning the next day, along with new ones, to his "in" basket till at last he exploded in a meeting and demanded to know who the practical joker was. The wild laughter that greeted his explosion didn't improve his temper at the moment, but it helped to clear the air.

Gradually the two schools of civil servant thought began to see the special merits of each other's systems, to work together, and to have mutual respect. This long history of international elbow-rubbing is one of the particular values of ILO to other parts of the UN. Newer agencies often have profited from its time-tested administrative advice. No other agency has had its wealth of experience.

Under the League and in the interregnum before the UN, ILO worked steadily to set up better conditions of employment for men and women, to prevent unemployment, to lower working hours. It gathered admirable labor statistics. The standards it recommended and worked for never won any international legal standing, but, gradually, bit by bit, they became realities—many of them, at any rate. The eight-hour day, for example, and the protection of women workers.

On the other hand, as time went on, it became clearer that the primary objectives of the labor movement could not be achieved in a vacuum. From the beginning, in 1919, ILO had had a unique "tripartite" worker-government-employer membership, but the focus of attention was on labor's welfare and problems, as distinct from those of the rest of the community. By time of World War II and even more by the time ILO entered the UN as a Specialized Agency its viewpoint had broadened. The emphasis turned to over-all increased productivity, in which labor should have a just share.

David A. Morse, Director-General of ILO since 1948, thinks of the change as "acceleration" or "implementation" of long-term ILO working plans. In a number of directions ILO has become more "operational."

For instance, in what might be called the diplomatic field, ILO was called upon some years ago to intercede in a dispute between the International Transport Workers Federation and the Government of Panama. Actually, the matter had come before the ILO Maritime Commission as far back as 1933, but dragged on without action till finally, in 1948, the seamen's organization threatened a boycott of certain ships flying the Panamanian flag. Its claim was that the ships were obsolete and had been transferred to registration in Panama to dodge taxes, currency regulations, safety rules and social and labor standards. ILO investigated, while the Transport Workers postponed the boycott. Then, from the investigation, ILO suggested a number of changes in Panama's maritime laws. The Government of Panama rather bitterly objected to parts of the ILO investigation, but in the end revised its laws pretty much to the satisfaction of the workers and the threat of boycott ended.

Mr. Morse recalls a more striking case that had its scene in Greece. Information came to the ILO Committee on Freedom of Association that a number of union leaders had been sentenced to death in Greece and were in early danger of execution. The Director-General promptly wrote the Greek Government a polite letter asking for names and descriptions of the men referred to, the crimes with which they were charged and the judgments rendered against them. The response to this letter at first denied that trade unionism had anything to do with the cases, insisting the men had been tried and sentenced to death for treason, but then it went on to say that the Greek Government had passed clemency measures which covered the men in question and they were therefore safe from execution, though imprisoned for life. It appeared, however, that other men in much the same position *had* been executed, and in labor circles ILO got credit for highly persuasive letter-writing. More important, the incident reflected the prestige of its Freedom of Association Committee as a protection for trade unionists throughout the free world.

In the more contemporary field of increasing productivity, ILO has spread out pretty widely, along with the rest of the Expanded Technical Assistance Program. Over half its field work is vocational training, and mostly training trainers. William Yalden-Thomson, Assistant Director-General in charge of Technical Assistance operations, defines the worth-while field man as one who can get the feel of local materials and teach natives of the locality to make the most of them. Also—and more important for ILO's purposes—one who has the knack of teaching natives how to teach other natives. ILO wants to get job-training going, in the most effective manner possible, but it also wants to get its experts out and on another job just as fast as the local people are trained well enough to take over for themselves.

The last paragraph sounds like Asia or South America. But probably ILO's most spectacular project so far has been the politically delicate business of Yugoslavia. As everyone knows, Yugoslav head man Marshal Tito is the first (and up to now only) leader of a Communist satellite country to break away from the Kremlin, carrying his nation with him and still professing Communist ideology. His country represents a wholly singular gray between the stark black and white of the world's political division today, depending on and to an extent promising to defend the one side, while still leaning toward the other philosophically.

Since the break with Moscow Tito has had no easy time either politically or economically. Earlier standard Communist efforts toward farm collectivization backfired and his industrial program stayed in low gear. Finally he came to ILO, saying, in effect: "We can build factories, but we can't find people to run them." What he wanted particularly was foremen, well trained in specific jobs.

Because of the political aspects, ILO foresaw fairly hideous trouble in the project, but it also saw a challenge worth accepting and went ahead.

The sometimes vaunted advantages of a dictatorship worked out in one way. ILO wanted very carefully selected trainees and Tito saw it got them, cutting every strand of red tape that interfered. The 370 men chosen were briefed with the greatest care to avoid friction between them and their politically different host-trainers, then were sent all over Europe—mainly to Western Germany, Sweden, Holland, France and Belgium. For precaution, ILO set up a rigid inspection system to operate during the training period in the various factories where the trainees were installed. ILO also sent to Yugoslavia from various European countries 350 veteran foremen to prepare the ground in Tito's factories for the return of the newly trained natives. Then ILO sat back to wait, in trepidation.

It was almost a disappointment, things went so smoothly. The Yugoslavs turned out to be eager beavers who loved every minute of their training and kept their instructors after hours asking pertinent questions. There wasn't a trace of political trouble. Factory managers liked the trainees' work so well that in a number of cases they asked permission to keep them on.

Perhaps the human payoff came with the disastrous floods that swept England and the Low Countries in 1952. The Yugoslav foremen-trainees in the Netherlands emptied their pockets of every guilder to help.

When the project was ended Tito requested another million dollars of ILO Technical Assistance to renew the training drive. Greece and Israel, taking notice, also asked for foreman-training aid.

A less spectacular but more typical piece of work was done by an ILO man in Haiti, who found out a way to tan local skins into very beautiful leather and taught his method to thirty Haitians. They picked up his evangelical enthusiasm and began spreading his technique to other trainees and trainers. Now there is every likelihood that the island will have a profitable small tanning industry where nothing of the sort existed before.

This is the kind of grass-roots, pay-as-you-go, one-thing-at-a-time development most ILO people believe in. They have had thirty-five years' experience in the ups and downs of international effort and their resultant philosophy is one of pretty adamant gradualism. They refused to give up when the League folded. They were flattered to death when the UN invited them to join the fold. After the United States Point Four program poured $66,000,000 into an Afghanistan hydroelectric irrigation dam project (the results of which one observer described as "something out of Evelyn Waugh—with about a hundred yards of usable road, electricity no one could read by and the rest confusion"), ILO imperturbably sent out a practical Greek who was expected to find out what the Afghans had the capacity and resources to do for themselves, then help guide them to make the most of both. The budget for the Greek was about $12,000 a year.

This is not to say that ILO keeps its head cautiously hidden in the sand. Once or twice, on the contrary, it has been found with its neck rather conspicuously stuck out. The Altiplano survey was such an occasion. Its categorical title was "Indigenous Population Survey" and a number of sparkling ideas were expected to dazzle forward-looking citizens once proceedings got under way. Actually, they *did* get under way to the extent that fourteen or fifteen ILO, FAO, WHO, UNESCO and UN experts spent four months studying the multi-thousand-feet-high Andean plateau of Bolivia, Peru and Ecuador that goes by the name of Altiplano. Here, at least a quarter of the earth's tin and a lot of other minerals make fabulous fortunes and periodic political revolutions for some people. But here, too, the "indigenous population," illiterate, diseased and poor beyond description, scratches out practically no living at all. ILO thought it might make a spectacular scene for pilot projects in a new way of life, teaching new skills to use on the old resources, educating, eradicating disease. And the preliminary survey, sparked by ILO, was considered something of a classic. But other Specialized Agencies that were expected to share the work and expense of a four-year program became reluctant, particularly after a sharp cut in the expected Technical Assistance funds, and the project at last report was uncertain, leaving ILO out on the limb with partial commitments that couldn't be carried on to any worth-while conclusions without the other Agencies' co-operation.

ILO stuck its neck out in another direction at about the same time. This particular protrusion happened in India. Privately owned textile and engineering industries asked ILO to supervise testing of a managerial technique called "productivity and payment by results." In the United States it is better known and argued over as the "incentive plan." The peculiar delicacy of this venture lay in the fact that in India employment at any sort of wage or pay is a kind of privilege that Occidentals do not understand. Somewhere between 40 and 50 per cent of the Indian adults able to work are normally unemployed, in any Western sense. They are in a permanent condition of unemployment, not expecting anything else. A regularly paid job of any sort for half the people is more or less in the dream world of those "You, too, can make $15,000 a year if" advertisements that sell correspondence courses in this country. Except that this half of the Indian population can't read.

The peculiar delicacy—and danger—of the venture was that it might destroy a few jobs. A very few—even six or eight or ten— would be enough to lose face for the labor unions. Yet they were willing to take the chance, and ILO embarked on the experiment, insisting only that both labor and management be in together on every step of the way. The object, of course, was increased productivity—an especially desperate need of India—and the risks seemed worth taking.

Preliminary results in the engineering field showed increases from 12.5 to 116 per cent; in textiles from 6 to 36 per cent.

This is the new "operational" or "accelerated" or "implementational" philosophy of ILO at work.

There is, ILO people like to feel, less disposition nowadays to send experts out into the field who come back and write elaborate reports that are "filed and forgotten." As an instance of the latter-day emphasis on concrete results, they suggest a minor project in Jordan. When it was brought up, ILO had doubts the Government of Jordan would be interested enough in the end to contribute its proper share. But an expert nevertheless was sent, though with specific instructions to find out the Government's attitude before getting the Agency too involved. To the surprise of Geneva headquarters, things began to pop almost immediately. The Government quickly agreed to the project and at once allotted land for buildings, the United Nations Relief and Works Agency came up with a $40,000 grant, the expert completed a foot-high pile of blueprints and before his return home learned that work had already started on construction—two and a half weeks after he set out.

This, ILO people felt, was action.

They like to cite seventy-three-year-old Sir Malcolm Darling as a similar example. Arriving in Pakistan on an ILO mission, he asked for transportation and got evasive replies. "Well," said Sir Malcolm, "if you haven't a jeep, give me a burro and let's go." Or, regarding another Pakistan mission, the anxiety of a male member over a female member who disapproved of Oriental religious discrimination against women: "The first week I was afraid she was going to start a religious war. The second week I was sure she'd win it."

Training, of course, is a vital function of many Specialized Agencies, particularly under the Technical Assistance Program. ILO's training is essentially vocational. Where, as at the famous proving ground in Pátzcuaro, Mexico, there is a combined effort by several agencies, ILO people try to keep their teachers in the strictly vocational channel, giving instruction in handicrafts, mechanical skills and the like. Reading and writing are up to UNESCO, farming to FAO, health to WHO.

Nevertheless, a dividing line is often hard to find. Ask an FAO expert at what point a tree goes out of FAO jurisdiction into something else. He may get fired with enthusiasm and find himself in carpentry before he knows it. Similarly, ILO, because it has as a long-time goal reasonable standards of living for all workers, finds itself hip-deep in a pretty world-wide movement for land reform. Land reform, of course, essentially means breaking up big absentee-ownership estates into smaller owner-operated farms. Historically, it is probably the most explosive political and economic issue known to man. Every conceivable political label has been attached to it, from Roman times and before, down through the Middle Ages, our own Civil War, present-day commotions in the Philippines, Asia and elsewhere. The enormous conflict over collectivization in Soviet Russia, in historical perspective, was merely an item in the long chronology. Whether in our day land is best farmed in small areas for philosophical reasons of personal ownership or in large areas for most economical use of machinery, for planning, etc., is a question that the experts argue at length. But ILO, like many other organizations, cannot fail to take an interest. Whichever way a decision goes, workers are involved.

Where once ILO made its greatest point in setting up standards, such as the eight-hour day, protection for women at work, industrial safety regulations, disability insurance and wage scales, it now makes greater effort to implement those standards. Most of its aims are already immortalized in beautifully written laws. The problem, as is particularly true with social security laws, is to guarantee proper administration.

The tendency has good exemplification in a minor branch of ILO's program. This is rehabilitation work and placement of persons disabled either in industry or by any other cause. Mr. A. A. Bennett, ILO expert in the field, made it dramatic with a very casual remark: "The United States, you know, has a very liberal definition of blindness."

People with more or less normal sight tend to think of blindness as a condition without qualification. We may say: "I'm practically blind." But we don't mean anything of the sort. When we really think of blindness, we think of the dark. Yet for the purposes of industrial employment, compensation and insurance there obviously have to be measurable degrees of vision impairment. In a negative kind of way it's nice to know that the United States has a liberal definition of blindness. It's also good to know that a strong UN organization like ILO watches over such matters without our asking.

Finally, ILO has one over-all competence that comes close to beggaring the competence of every other organ of the UN. Worldwise, it knows more about manpower than any other organization. What mankind has the capacity to accomplish ILO knows better than anyone else. The knowledge some day should prove useful.

What the UN Does about Money

Although the UN and all its Specialized Agencies operate on an annual budget hardly greater than that of the New York City Department of Sanitation (which, for some reason, is the favorite comparison), and talk of poverty is as sad in the Secretariat Building as it is in any normal American household, two of the UN's Specialized Agencies do have money to play around with, if the expression doesn't sound too careless. And the sums have a billion-dollar flavor markedly in contrast with other UN outlays.

These agencies are the International Monetary Fund (known as the Fund) and the International Bank for Reconstruction and Development (known as the Bank).

Workings of the Fund are impossibly mysterious to nonfinancial minds (like ours) that can barely understand how to balance a checkbook. Long, long ago most national currencies had their value related to the value of gold, and even then fluctuations in exchange (or relative value of one national currency to another) were fre-

quent and erratic. Shrewd men who understood such matters made
money out of them. Nowadays, with most of the gold in the world
underground at Fort Knox, the problem of understanding is even
more intricate.

There are complicated exchange restrictions enforced by governments practically everywhere, and many currencies have different
valuations domestically and abroad. Partly because of such restrictions, one country owing another country money because of unequal
imports and exports may have great difficulty making payment. By
making American dollars, Belgian francs and British pounds sterling
available, the Fund eases such short-term crises. It also helps member countries, when possible and beneficial, to keep their currencies
at par, by the same method of putting up dollars, francs or sterling.
Up to the beginning of 1953 the Fund had exchanged $896,408,380
of these relatively strong currencies for the weaker currencies of
some twenty-two countries to help with their international financial
problems.

Aside from advancing a monetary helping hand, the Fund has
been active in urging relaxation of exchange restrictions. Admitting
that these "may for the time being have to exist in many countries,"
it still hopes to help its fifty-four members work toward a "relatively
free state of international trade and payments."

Further than this specific purpose, the Fund's Articles of Agreement require member governments to adhere to the high standards
of conduct in financial and foreign exchange affairs set up by the
organization. Through constant consultation with governments the
Fund feels it is definitely improving the international code of ethics
in the exchange field.

The Fund's staff of financial and economic technicians, gathered
from thirty-one countries, is constantly at work gathering and
analyzing data on the shifting economic and financial scene, and
these findings are available to members, Moreover, Fund experts
have directly helped members to combat inflation, improve credit
policies, draft new banking laws, establish foreign exchange budgets and study the financial aspects of development programs.

The Fund receives no financial support from the UN, which might interest some readers in the question, where it gets eight hundred-odd million dollars with which to do business. As a matter of fact, its assets are more than ten times that figure.

This, very roughly, is how it works. Each member government is assigned a quota, either in the original Articles of Agreement or as it joins the Fund. The quota determines the member's voting power and also the amount of foreign exchange, if eligible, it is entitled to buy from the Fund. To join, a government must subscribe an amount equal to its quota, partly in gold and partly in its own currency. The quotas vary from Panama's $500,000 to $2,750,000,000 for the United States. Sales of exchange are subject to a service charge of three-fourths per cent, payable in gold or partly in gold and partly in the member's own currency. This service charge has been the Fund's chief source of income.

The Fund's purposes, of course, are high: "to facilitate the expansion . . . of international trade, and to contribute thereby to the promotion and maintenance of high levels of employment and real income and to the development of the productive resources of all members" by promoting "international monetary co-operation through a permanent institution which provides the machinery for consultation and collaboration on international monetary problems."

Yet, when a major money policy change, such as currency devaluation, is about to take place, smart operators obviously can cash in on advance information. Since it's unavoidable that a number of officials know what's going on, there is always the chance of a leak. The Fund is particularly proud that no leak has occurred in connection with any of its operations.

The International Bank for Reconstruction and Development was set up more or less in tandem with the Monetary Fund. Some board members work with both institutions and the two share an office building in Washington. (They are the only Specialized Agencies with headquarters in the U.S.) It's even necessary for a country or territory to become a member of the Fund before it's eligible to become a member of the Bank.

But their functions are clearly distinct. The Fund is intended to help keep national currencies stable, so that industry, trade and agriculture have the confidence and favorable financial atmosphere to expand themselves and thereby improve the people's living standards. Its effect on the individual is indirect. But the Bank is intended to lend money directly for the reconstruction, the establishment or expansion of industry and agriculture. The effect of its operations in making jobs and improving living standards is concrete and immediate, visible to anyone.

The idea, of course, is not to give money away and therefore experienced credit men weigh the probabilities of repayment before any loan is made. But for a banker with imagination it must be far more cheerful deliberation than in the case of an ordinary commercial loan, because one of the chief considerations always is the effect of the loan itself. Will it help the country or the area to become more productive? Will it help balance the economy? Will it help to make jobs that are permanent? Will it help to make people more content? If it will, other things being reasonably advantageous, then it probably will be repaid and is worth making. There aren't many Wall Street men or bankers in small towns who can afford to think this way, but it's the fundamental and in the long run very practical philosophy of the Bank.

Before the Marshall Plan went into effect in Europe it used its available half-billion dollars of investment money to help in the reconstruction of the continent's ravaged industry. Now its attention is turned mainly toward less highly developed countries in other parts of the world. The place-names of its investments read like an atlas—Mexico, Brazil, India, Colombia, Iraq, Turkey, Australia, Uruguay, Ethiopia, Thailand, Nicaragua, Iceland, the Belgian Congo, Paraguay, Southern Rhodesia, Pakistan, Peru, Iran, Ceylon and also countries closer home. Loans to date total a billion and a half dollars.

Of that total the largest amount went for reconstruction, reflecting the urgent needs of Europe in the immediate postwar years. The second largest amount reflects the newer phase of the Bank's activities, development—in this case, electric power development. Third is transportation; fourth, agriculture and forestry; and fifth, industry.

One loan to India is an attractive example of the Bank's investment policy. The sum was $18,500,000 and it was paid in April, 1950, to aid the Bokar-Konar project—a combination electric power flood control irrigation and increased water supply development similar to our own Tennessee Valley plan.

The scene is the Damodar Valley, through which flows the Konar River. Bokar and Konar are two new cities springing up on the river, Konar at the site of a dam being built with the help of Bank funds, Bokar twelve miles downstream where a steam electric plant is under construction, also with the help of Bank funds. About 4,500 people have been working to build the communities out of what was useless jungle, building not only houses (out of concrete block, incidentally, instead of the traditional mud), but also roads. The area had been inaccessible before.

The new houses have electricity, running water and adequate sanitary facilities—none of which had been known in this region of India. Bokar and Konar offer regular jobs—something rare anywhere in India. And clearing of the jungle offers new tillable land, part of which is to be taken over by the farmers whose land will be inundated when the dam is in operation. But there has been a gradual migration both to the new farming land and the cities from surrounding areas.

Engineers are instructing the Indians in construction and operation of both the dam and the steam electric plant, which is scheduled for completion in 1953. India's Damodar Valley Corporation, a public agency patterned after the American TVA, which is conducting the whole program, also is responsible for setting up model farms in the new farming areas where the paddy farmers learn modern agricultural techniques, such as contour plowing and terracing to prevent erosion, use of improved manures.

The Damodar Valley is rich in mineral resources and the addition of the Bokar electric plant's 150,000 kilowatts will surely raise and make cheaper the output of coal, which up to now has been mined largely by hand. Increased power will benefit the steel and associated industries already established in the valley and develop new ones, such as fertilizer plants, cement plants and locomotive repair shops. Production of many other minerals is expected to go along with the effects already mentioned of added electric power.

There are dozens of other probable results. If all the good effects eventuate the Bokar-Konar project might well turn out to be the inspiration for a whole new way of Indian life.

This is not by any means to hint that the Bank would be responsible for bringing the Indian people out of centuries of abject poverty. Its loan is only a part of the financing. Incentive for the project was Indian. And its direction is in the hands of Indian Government officials. But the Bank, nevertheless, has helped and in doing so has shown the nature of its aims.

The fact that the Bank merely helped with its loan and cannot take credit for all the good that may result parallels a point that its president, Eugene R. Black, often emphasizes in connection with our part in the European postwar recovery. He chides Americans who say our ten- or twelve-billion-dollar contribution did the job, stating that 90 per cent of the capital for reconstruction came from Europe itself. Then he goes on to insist that outside aid cannot be the complete answer to economic development anywhere, quoting one of the conclusions reached at the Commonwealth Economic Conference in London late in 1952: "The major sources of capital to promote development must come from within each country. . . . Capital from outside will then find a fruitful basis on which to work."

A few other quotes from Mr. Black give a good notion of the Bank's thinking.

The problem of lifting living standards, he says, "is not just to provide capital, but to help create conditions and skills for using it effectively. . . .

"Farm production is fundamental in the underdeveloped countries. Agriculture is the chief economic activity in most of them, and the pressure of growing populations on available food supply is one of their major problems. Moreover, productive agriculture is usually a basic requisite for ultimate industrialization. Farm productivity must rise if man-power is to be released for industry; farm earnings must increase if a healthy market is to be provided for local manufactures. . . .

"In many underdeveloped countries the lack of basic facilities . . . means that industrialization must begin modestly with small and light industries; but it is extremely difficult . . . for the Bank to assess the comparative economic value . . . of many small industrial enterprises. . . .

"We are particularly glad when we are able to finance not merely one isolated project, but several projects which will have a cumulative effect on a country's economic life. In Ethiopia, for instance, we have made separate loans for highways, for telephone and radio communication, and for a development bank. The roads should give farmers and stock-raisers an incentive to added production through easier access to markets; the development bank should be able to make loans for processing plants which will increase the earnings from Ethiopia's agricultural exports; and new communications, making possible the dissemination of market information and the control of freight shipments, should greatly aid the country's domestic and international commerce in agricultural products."

It was said earlier that a banker with imagination must find it more cheerful to deliberate over a loan of the International Bank kind than an ordinary commercial one, because one of the chief considerations always is the effect of the loan itself. But it must not be forgotten—and the Bank does not forget—that one of the effects of lending is on lending itself. The Bank objects to very long-term cheap loans, not because it wants to deny aid where it's needed, but because such loans tend to demoralize the whole financial structure. They imply a lack of interest in repayment on the part of both parties and end by reducing the chances of repayment. To grants in aid, called just that, the Bank has no objection. But if it's a loan, it should be treated as a loan, and paid off, on time, with full interest.

In the case of real loans, the Bank, like any other self-respecting financial institution, takes a paternal interest in the borrower, gives good advice in every way possible, and sends him customers.

What the UN Does about the Mail

As the largest of the Specialized Agencies in point of members (ninety-three), the next oldest and perhaps the most successful international organ existing today, the Universal Postal Union takes very little nonsense from anyone. A few sentences from the 1952 UPU report will give an idea:

In 1951, relations between the United Nations and the Universal Postal Union developed regularly and without interruption. . . . The Union sent representatives to several meetings of the United Nations, the agenda of which contained items likely to be of interest to the UPU. . . . On the other hand, the UPU continued its previous practice of declining invitations to sessions which were of no interest to it. . . . For its part, the Union invited the United Nations to send representatives to the May-June session of the executive and Liaison Commission. The United Nations accepted this invitation. . . .

An attitude like this of rather aloof equality by the part toward the whole suggests a solid amount of self-esteem. And there is no doubt that UPU has grounds for it.

It is easy enough to be romantic about the business of carrying mail. Its history goes back to the beginning of writing. When messages could be written and read, the next logical step was someone to carry them: viz., the postman.

The first regular postal system on record was set up in 500 B.C. by Darius the Persian, who used relays of horsemen, in the manner of our own nineteenth-century Pony Express, to carry messages throughout his huge empire. Julius Caesar organized a mail service during his conquest of Britain that got letters to Rome in twenty-six days. In 1800 it took thirty days.

Until the year 1635 mail service was largely a royal prerogative

or at least a private privilege. Britain's postmaster, Thomas Wither-
ings, that year established a public post between London and Edin-
burgh. But then, and for a long time thereafter, the system was to
charge by distance rather than weight and a person sending a
letter overseas might have a choice of three different prices, depending on the route the ship took. He was never too sure of delivery, either.

The postage stamp was not a midnight stroke of individual
genius. In seventeenth-century Paris there was a local postal service
costing a sou per letter. The sender paid and got a receipt, which
he sent along with the letter. It was from that practice that the
postage stamp finally developed in the nineteenth century.

England and France concluded the first postal treaty in 1670, by
which England supplied semiweekly packets across the Channel
and France carried the mail overland to Lyons. But all over the
world communication by letter continued to be helter-skelter and
unreliable through the eighteenth and much of the nineteenth centuries. With the great expansion of trade in the nineteenth century,
many additional treaties between countries were signed, but there
remained irritating differences in rates and methods of handling,
and pressure mounted for international regulation.

The United States suggested the first conference to find a solution.
It met in Paris in 1863. But the American Civil War interfered, as
did the Franco-Prussian War of 1870-1871. (Incidentally, it was
during the latter conflict that airmail first became known, with a
pigeon-and-balloon service out of besieged Paris to Tours.) And
it wasn't until 1874 that an international congress at Berne, Switzerland, agreed on a plan to bring order to world mail delivery.

This agreement, which was called the International Postal Convention, provided for uniformity in treatment of correspondence, for
simplification of accounts and for reduction of rates, which were to
be calculated on weight rather than distance. It also provided for
the establishment of what in 1875 was called the General Postal
Union and in 1878 changed its name to the Universal Postal Union,
the present UN Specialized Agency.

But it was UPU as an independent entity that did the job of

setting the world's mail delivery to rights. Hence its attitude of well-deserved self-esteem.

The job UPU does is almost incredibly vast. Under its aegis about sixty billion letters a year are handled inexpensively and with dispatch. So smooth is the operation that not one person in a thousand has any idea how it's done.

Probably because the operation *is* so vast, the basic principle behind it is exceedingly simple; it has to be. The basic principle is to regard all member states as a single territory. Since UPU's member states and territories (ninety-three of them) for any practical purpose comprise the whole world, this means that national borders are disregarded. Like radio signals and the weather, the mail knows no frontiers. And, being realists in their way, Soviet leaders recognize the fact. UPU is one of the three Specialized Agencies with which they stayed after leaving all the others.

The single-territory principle imposes a duty on each member state to transmit foreign mails entrusted to it by the best means it uses for its own mails. Hence every country has access to the railway, shipping and airmail services of every other country in the world, at uniform rates and with uniform treatment.

The figure of sixty billion letters a year does not mean only letters moving from country to country. That figure is probably not much over two billion at present. The sixty billion letters are the total handled both internationally and internally by member countries. UPU does not interfere with internal practices of members, though its advice is available through the International Bureau at Berne, Switzerland, and has had effect in promoting efficiency. (Circulars requesting information which is later published in other circulars give a hint in their homely titles, such as: "Two Features of Mailbags" and "Use of Bicycles in Rural Areas.") What it does is collect and publish information of all kinds relating to postal service, issue lists of air and steamer services and act as an office for settling international accounts.

This last function is one that puzzles many people, how any accounting system could keep track of two billion items scattered around among ninety-odd countries and territories. Obviously, UPU makes no attempt to balance books to the penny. What happens is that every three years member countries compare a month's transactions one with another and pay off the differences through UPU.

Not that the business is done casually. One of the duties of the International Bureau at Berne is to adjust disputes among members over such payments. A UPU Report immortalizes one such argument in nearly six pages of type, with twenty-two clauses and many more subclauses, reflecting much correspondence, sharp legal thought and weighty deliberation—all over the sum of 5.12 gold francs, or about $1.75.

In addition to adjusting disputes, the International Bureau stands ready to answer questions of any member as to practices that affect the other members.

A standard requirement of UPU members is that they follow regulations in handling eight types of "ordinary mail"—letters, single and reply-paid post cards, commercial papers, printed matter, raised print for the blind (the 1952 UPU Congress voted for free transmission of such literature), samples of merchandise, small packets and phono-post articles, such as phonograph records.

There are seven other postal services outlined in agreements supplementing the basic Postal Convention. UPU members have to observe the agreements only if their governments have ratified them. The services cover insured letters and boxes, parcel post, money orders, cash on delivery packages, postal checks, collection orders and subscriptions to periodicals.

The UPU Congress meets every five years to revise the Universal Postal Convention (as the International Postal Convention was renamed in 1947). In 1952 two of the more interesting changes were a 50 per cent reduction in rates on all newspapers, books and magazines sent abroad, and amplification of a scheme to permit payment in national currency, at local post offices, for subscriptions to foreign newspapers and magazines, with low-rate mailing rates. The United Nations Educational, Scientific and Cultural Organization had urged these changes.

Although UPU does not interfere in the workings of its members' domestic postal services, it has within recent years, through its International Bureau, added to the organization facilities for the exchange of technical information among all the member postal administrations.

The International Bureau supplies member postal administrations with the many millions of international reply coupons that are used each year to facilitate correspondence between countries.

It is also the philatelist's friend. It receives stamps of all kinds from all member countries and territories and is required, under the Convention, to distribute them to all other members. In one year it handles 2,500 different kinds of stamps.

What the UN Does about the Weather

It hasn't, of course, been true for many years, as Mark Twain complained, that no one does anything about the weather. Meteorologists have done a great deal about the weather. A lot of their work has been done in strange and lonely places, remote from the so-called civilized world, and almost all of it has been negative, in the sense that it has consisted of observation rather than constructive action.

Nevertheless, the observation has resulted in better short-term forecasts and more detailed patterns of wind, rain and storm now available have made modern aviation possible—even if it's still not practicable to plan a picnic a week in advance, and even if farmers' almanacs are the only institutions brave enough to prognosticate next spring's climate.

On the positive side, there has been enough experimentation for meteorological realists to say flatly that rain-making is a scientific possibility, provided we are willing to pay the price and make the equipment necessary to work our will on the millions of tons of air hanging over our heads. It is even possible to make rain without too much cost and without fantastic new mechanisms, under just the right conditions, locally, and now. Airplane spraying of clouds with silver iodide or dry ice has done it.

But the main meteorological work has been and remains trying to find out what weather has been and what it is now. Benjamin Franklin had ideas about wind patterns that gave a good deal of inspiration to later students of weather. We can say with assurance —from much detailed observation—that weather travels generally from west to east. And we can say with equal assurance that this is the reason why Soviet Russia remained a supporter and co-operative member of the UN's World Meteorological Organization long after leaving all but two other of the Specialized Agencies. She got more out of it than the Western countries. Oddly enough, however, and the technicians have no explanation, a good deal of winter weather moves westward from Siberia.

But these are generalities that don't help much in specific situations. For instance, in the Allied invasion of Europe during World War II it would have been enormously valuable to have month-ahead predictions, even for the Infantry. But the best meteorologists could do for the Air Force was a twelve-hour forecast, followed by a three-hour jump-up. One of the things WMO officials like to emphasize is that a weather report never says what the weather will be, only what it is. From present conditions, accurately reported, experts can make fair estimates of the near future. These are called forecasts.

The trouble is that there aren't enough modern weather stations, manned by well-trained technicians, in all the meteorologically important parts of all the world. There isn't enough radio equipment. And therefore the day-to-day global weather pattern is anything but complete. Since aviation has become so important, air currents are a matter of particular concern. Range of planes has been increased so vastly that most of them can fly around or over storms, or choose a new destination within a thousand miles. But winds, though they have a generally easterly direction, are fickle at all altitudes. Learning more about them, and how to cope with them, is a matter of great moment to WMO.

Weather has a connection with agriculture that no farmer ever failed to see. But large-scale agricultural enterprises, like Hawaiian pineapple growing, have turned increasingly to modern meteorology for their forecasting needs. There is less reliance on the old-time farmer's instinct about rainfall and more on statistical records of the past, along with attention to current indications.

In Syria farmers have wheat harvest in May and look anxiously to the sky for clouds that may drop a little water to fill out the wheat buds. But the French, on their departure, left no weather data behind them, on which to make even the most general predictions. In the Judean hills, where there are six months of sunshine a year, the farmers want to know when to expect rain, but the only radio receiving sets are in the coffee shops. In Iraq there is need of irrigation, but the farmers don't want to use the precious dammed-up waters if it's going to rain. And they don't know when it's going to rain.

As the latest of the Specialized Agencies (it came into being April 4, 1951, though its predecessor, the International Meteorological Organization, stemmed back to 1853), WMO has had less opportunity to boast of definite achievements than some of the others. But the problems it faces and some of the projects it proposes to carry out are a good deal more fascinating than the average layman might suppose.

Aside from rainfall, frost and such weather matters of interest to farmers, there are insects. Locusts, for example, travel with the winds. They also breed according to moisture conditions. Hence they are a fit subject for meteorology and a WMO expert was invited to the Middle East to help in the fight against them. In Baghdad he got a request for WMO to do something about non-migratory insect pests, which was a bit harder for a weatherman.

WMO is co-operating with the UN Education, Scientific and Cultural Organization (UNESCO) on arid zone research. Since the dry belt extends entirely around the world (even through Haiti) from about 25 to 35 degrees North, the value of increasing its productivity is easy to appreciate. WMO's particular researches are in: sources of energy (wind and sun especially); the use of dew; the possibilities of artificial rain.

Another large-scale idea that appeals to some WMO officials, and that would affect agriculture, is a climatological survey of all of Africa. On a smaller scale, but still important to a very large area, is the hope of establishing in Afghanistan a rainfall observation post for the Upper Nile River. Such a plan as this last one depends in the first place on a request from the country involved. This, of course, is true of all Technical Assistance programs.

WMO works closely with the Food and Agriculture Organization, as one would expect. In some ways its co-operation, as one also would expect, is perhaps even more important to the International Civil Aviation Organization. Much of the proposed work is too technical for useful mention here, but one interesting task already has been attended to. This was defining the point meteorologically at which an airplane ought to attempt a forced landing on water.

A couple of other interesting jobs are: (1) preparing an international cloud atlas picturing all the kinds of clouds that appear over the various parts of the earth and (2) working up global charts of thunderstorm frequency and distribution. The latter involves helping to perfect a mechanism for counting flashes of lightning.

A radical idea for future thought and experiment that has nothing to do with aviation, agriculture or ships at sea, but does appeal to the imagination, is concerned with architecture. It has been talked of in Israel. The notion is that the temperature and wind measurements of meteorology could well be taken into account in the construction and siting of houses. Judicious use of such knowledge might result in a new sort of "indoor climating."

Meanwhile, the practical work of WMO is directed toward training technicians and advising governments that request help in modernizing their systems of weather observation and reporting. There were half a dozen Technical Assistance projects confirmed for 1953, with a total budget of $75,000.

One advantage WMO has over some of the other Specialized Agencies is an international code of reporting that obviates language difficulties. A Rumanian girl wanted to apply for a job in the weather bureau of Israel. No one in the office could understand Rumanian and she had no other language—which in almost any other occupation would have meant an impasse. But in this case she merely walked over to the map and plotted the weather on it, without error, from cabled information on the desk—not sent in the Rumanian language. She got the job and later learned Israeli.

What the UN Does for Telecommunication

The word "telecommunication" looks formidable and is not the easiest one in the world to pronounce. From an academic point of view it isn't even a very legitimate word, since it's half Greek and half Latin. But the aim in coining it is clear enough—to gather in one word the name for a number of ways to send and receive messages. These are chiefly the telegraph, the telephone and radio, but just to be on the safe side the definition includes "visual or electromagnetic systems." The Greek prefix "tele" merely means "far-off."

It took very little time after Samuel Morse invented the telegraph for European countries to put it to use. And they promptly found it necessary to make international agreements about standardized operation, kinds of apparatus and collection and accounting of rates. The first agreement came in 1850, between Germany and Austria, others quickly followed and in 1865 twenty countries signed a treaty at Paris, which created the International Telegraph Union to handle all the problems.

Radio was first used (this might be forgotten by some who do not remember a time when the air was free of commercials) as a safeguard for ships at sea. Radio and SOS were practically synonymous in the public mind. But even in those simple days it quickly became apparent that international regulations were necessary to standardize signals and define responsibilities. At a conference in 1906 at Berlin twenty-seven countries accepted the principle that it was a duty to answer a ship's call for help, either from shore or from another ship. This conference set up the International Radio-telegraph Union. And in 1934 this Union joined the original International Telegraph Union to form the International Telecommunication Union, which thus has the longest organizational history of the UN Specialized Agencies. It's also the second largest in point of members, with ninety-two countries or territories on the roster, two as associates. Only the Postal Union has more.

The telegraph and telephone have been around long enough not to demand anything very revolutionary in the way of international regulation nowadays—at least in peacetime. Perhaps as a result, it has been intimated that ITU turned into and remained for many years something of a European gentlemen's club. No American got in until 1945.

But radio is a different and much more exciting matter, even though the conflicts involve electronic objectives and techniques that are well over most nontechnical heads. In a figurative, as well as literal, sense, one expert pointed out, radio is the most sensitive area of the modern world.

In a 1927 conference of the International Radiotelegraph Union (before it merged with the International Telegraph Union to form the present ITU), the nations reached an agreement not to interfere with existing radio stations. That meant they agreed to stay off transmitting frequencies assigned to stations already in existence.

This was advantageous for American radio, because we were pioneers in the field and had pre-empted most of the desirable frequencies. But it could hardly increase our popularity abroad.

The 1927 agreement was reaffirmed in 1932 when the radio and telegraph unions decided to merge into ITU. After the actual merger, in 1934, ITU had headquarters at Berne, Switzerland, and authorized frequency assignments came to be known as the "Berne List." Qualification for listing depended on two things: (1) date of first use of a frequency by a station and (2) date of notification to ITU.

So far so good. This was the day of relatively low frequencies and things went along smoothly enough. But suddenly the day of high frequencies dawned—short-wave radio. And, to put it mildly, the situation changed.

In 1939 the Russians filed application for short-wave stations at every five kilocycles along the spectrum. They made little effort to justify their applications by setting up or even by faking stations, though here and there something of that sort happened. All they did was attempt to take over practically the whole upper range of frequencies by means of a little paper work.

Actually, in 1938 the spectrum had been charted only up to 200,-000 kilocycles and it wasn't till an ITU conference at Atlantic City in 1947 that the new importance of short-wave was recognized by extending the table of frequency allocations up to 10,500,000 kilocycles.

At this 1947 Atlantic City conference the United States took the lead in an effort to change the method of allocating frequencies. The practical purpose, of course, was to outflank the Russian paper maneuver, but to everyone except the Soviet bloc the proposals seemed reasonable. Mainly, they involved junking the old date-of-first-use-date-of-notification system in favor of more pragmatic questions, such as the working condition of both sending and receiving equipment, and whether or not the station asking a frequency allocation really was in operation. A kind of international court for radio allocations was to be set up (International Frequency Registration Board) and a world conference at Geneva was to make out a basic list of allocations from which to start work—and which the Russians would have to accept.

The Russians did not accept. They resisted, and went right on resisting.

Finally, late in 1951, ITU held an Extraordinary Administrative Radio Conference at Geneva which decided to override the Russians and put the Atlantic City proposals into effect. The international court for allocations (IFRB), as a result, is now in operation, and the Russians, at last reports, were still resisting.

An official brochure about ITU diplomatically says the IFRB "will record frequency assignments made by the various countries, and advise ITU members with a view to operating the maximum number of radio channels in those portions of the spectrum where harmful interference may occur." Granted understanding of electronics, it might be interesting to know how such advice works out.

Despite conflicts, ITU remained one of the few fields where international co-operation still obtained after the schism between East and West. And, according to eyewitness reports, it wasn't the belligerent sort of "co-operation" represented in the General Assembly and various conferences, but the sort marked by a daily, courteous "Good morning."

The reason for this, of course, is that radio signals are no more barred or hindered by frontiers than is the weather. And that, without some effective agreement among nations about the use of frequencies, confusion in the ether might be even more extreme than it is in the political council chambers. Such chaos would be just as harmful to one side as the other.

ITU is assigned 1 per cent of the Technical Assistance Program funds—about $200,000—and in 1953 had about half a dozen projects in the field. Most of these were concerned with showing countries how to improve their telephone and telegraph systems, or reassessing their radio setups. There were also fellowships for training in communications. These were awarded only to electronics engineers or applicants of similar technical background.

What the UN Does for Civil Aviation

The tasks that most Specialized Agencies face, Herculean though they are, at least have a long historical background. Food production, health, learning, finance, mail service, even telegraphic communication are all activities in which men have had many years or many centuries of experience.

The tasks that the International Civil Aviation Organization faces are just as Herculean and brand-new at the same time. As a major factor in transportation, international civil aviation did not exist till after World War II. It was the war itself, with its cost-be-hanged demands for fast transport to all the corners of the globe, that made international civil aviation what it is today. True, in the five years from 1934 to 1939 air route mileage doubled and miles flown tripled, to a figure of 300,000,000 miles a year. But, during the war, Air Transport Command planes alone flew twice that distance in a single month!

Although ICAO must answer questions that were never asked before the last war, those questions began to make themselves heard right after World War I, when the first commercial air service was established between London and Paris, in 1919. The two hop-skip-and-jump crossings of the Atlantic that same year helped to draw attention to the questions. The 1919 Peace Conference took note and its Aeronautical Commission drew up an agreement known as the Paris Air Convention. This attempted to set up uniform technical regulations and to perfect air navigation. But probably its most important content was a formulation of what has remained the fundamental principle of international air law: that each nation's sovereignty extends to the air above it. This means, of course, that the planes of one country may not fly to the airfields of another country, or over that country, without express agreement between them.

In 1927 Pan American Airways began its overseas career with scheduled flights across the narrow sea between Key West, Florida, and Havana, Cuba. This led to a Pan American Convention in 1929 similar to the Paris Convention. But it wasn't till 1944 that the volume of air traffic became formidable enough to make broadly international action an obvious necessity.

The great volume of air traffic was still military in 1944, of course, but aviation people were looking to a future of air-minded travelers after hostilities ceased. They knew that on a commercial basis the world-wide system of navigational and meteorological facilities that the military had set up would be almost prohibitively expensive. They knew, too, that many political and economic conflicts forgotten during the alliance of war would inevitably pop up in peacetime. And that there were innumerable legal questions that had never been settled internationally. So, in 1944, fifty-two Allied and neutral nations met in Chicago to discuss what might be done. From that meeting, eventually, came the International Civil Aviation Organization, officially born April 4, 1947.

Between 1945 and 1947 there was an interim organization abbreviated as PICAO. One of its members was Spain, and Franco's dictatorship was not welcome in the UN or, at that time, in its Specialized Agencies. To complete negotiations for association with the UN as a Specialized Agency, ICAO's first Assembly had to pass an amendment to its constitution which had the effect of dropping Spain from membership. Oddly enough, at the same Assembly, Italy, an ex-Axis state, was accepted for membership. (In 1950 the UN's prohibition of Spanish membership in Specialized Agencies was rescinded, and Spain rejoined the organization.)

The work of ICAO breaks down into three main categories: air navigation, air transport and legal matters.

Starting with the last, the committee in charge aims to build up a body of international air law, by agreement among nations and by co-operation with other international organizations trying to unify and codify international law. It has tried to get recognition, on an international basis, of property rights in aircraft, even when they cross frontiers. And it struggles to straighten out such difficult questions as the legal status of an aircraft commander and the liability of an air carrier to passengers.

The Air Transport Committee is concerned with commercial matters like payments for the use of airports and navigational facilities, international airmail, insurance, taxation, gathering statistics. Under it a unit with the awkward title of "Division on Facilitation of International Air Transport" struggles to improve and standardize customs, immigration and other such procedures that have tended to keep planes expensively on the ground longer than necessary—and passengers waiting, which is more important to the average traveler.

But it is the work of the first committee, on air navigation, that has most general interest. Dr. Edward Warner, president of the ICAO Council, pointed out obstacles to its aims in these words:

[Air transport] requires, among other things, a network of air navigation aids extending almost from pole to pole. . . . Some must be installed where the touch of metal to the ungloved finger is an almost fatal error; and others where sweat-blurred eyes and sweat-slippery hands are a constant threat to precise adjustments. . . . They are needed in the wealthiest areas of the world; but also in the poorest; and obviously, but ironically and painfully, it happens that the installations which are most difficult to make and most costly to maintain, because of remoteness or of climatic and geographical conditions, are very commonly located in the territories of the governmental authorities which would be least able to bear even moderate expenses for such purpose.

Yet, he adds:

The safe and regular movement of aircraft depends upon unbroken perfection in the performance of certain services. It is not sufficient that radio communications be perfectly operated at 90 per cent of the aeronautical ground stations of the world, if the equipment of the remaining 10 per cent is worn out or neglected or inattentively operated.

To fill some of the gaps mentioned in Dr. Warner's statement, ICAO appointed a Joint Support Committee. Under it the first collective action was to establish a floating network of weather stations in the North Atlantic. The thirteen stations agreed on in 1946 were revised downward in 1949 to ten. These were served by twenty-five vessels, of various nations, in rotation. These vessels not only radioed weather and navigation guidance to aircraft, but also figured in some thrilling rescues at sea.

One that happened in 1947 won wide attention. An unscheduled flying boat, the *Bermuda Sky Queen*, ran out of fuel and landed in mid-ocean with sixty-nine passengers aboard. The vessel at Station C, U.S. Guard Cutter *Bibb*, in spite of thirty-foot-high seas, saved all the passengers and crew.

A different sort of aid was given a plane flying westward from the Azores. Bucking headwinds and turbulent weather, it lost the use of most of its navigational radio equipment and ran low on fuel, but managed to "home" on the weather station vessel. The pilot, with a low fuel supply and reports of more bad weather ahead, thought an attempt to reach Newfoundland by dead reckoning was a poor risk and wanted to ditch his plane by the surface vessel. But the vessel persuaded him to wait, got in touch with an eastbound plane and persuaded its pilot to change course, rendezvous at the station, then lead the first plane into Newfoundland.

The ocean station vessels also have made many rescues for disabled surface ships. But perhaps the most useful thing about them is that they provide a fine sense of security for pilots, who know they are there always, ready to help. Often enough that sense of security has saved a ditching. A plane in trouble will make for the nearest station vessel. Reaching it safely, the pilot will regain confidence and continue on to the nearest land, knowing his course is being plotted and help will be sent if he gets into further difficulty.

The Air Navigation Commission as a whole, under which the Joint Support Committee arranged for these oceangoing weather stations, has the duty of recommending all sorts of international standards and practices that will improve air navigation. Its interest and work are concerned with a wide variety of largely technical matters—airworthiness, accident investigation, air routes and ground aids, meteorology, search and rescue, communications, rules of the air and air traffic control, personnel licensing.

The procedure is for ICAO technical divisions to work out suggestions which the Air Navigation Commission considers, then presents to the ICAO Council. If the Council adopts them, they are passed on to member governments. Then, unless a majority of the member governments *disapprove*, they go into effect. This means that every member is bound to abide by them or notify ICAO of any discrepancy in its own practices. Out of the first dozen sets of new standards adopted by the Council and submitted to member states, twelve went into effect.

What's to Come

These are the ten Specialized Agencies already in existence (plus UNICEF). Two more are planned, but not yet realized. One of these two is the International Trade Organization (ITO), conceived of as the third member of a triumvirate, including the Bank and the Fund, to aid international trade.

For ITO, breaking through the international trade barrier of tariffs will be a paramount task. While establishment of the agency has been postponed indefinitely, the tariff task has been attacked with considerable success in three conferences (Geneva, 1947; Annecy, 1949; and Torquay, 1950-1951). These resulted in a treaty called the General Agreement on Tariffs and Trade (GATT), put into effect on a provisional basis by thirty-four countries. It covers 55,000 tariff rates.

The other Specialized Agency still to come is the Inter-Governmental Maritime Consultative Organization (IMCO). In a rough way, it will parallel the International Civil Aviation Organization, promoting international co-operation in maritime navigation, encouraging maximum use of safety measures and seeking removal of shipping restrictions and discriminations.

The budgets of the Specialized Agencies now operating and which require support from their members (the Bank and Fund are self-supporting) range from a few hundred thousand to eight or nine million dollars a year, with an over-all total of about forty million dollars a year. UNESCO, World Health Organization and the International Labour Organisation have the heaviest regular expenditures, the World Meteorological Organization the least. In addition to their regular over-all income of forty millions, eight of the Specialized Agencies are allotted varying shares of the Technical Assistance fund.

Technical Assistance began with a relatively small appropriation by the UN itself ($288,000 in 1949). In 1950 fifty member nations pledged an additional sum of twenty million dollars, above the UN appropriation, for an eighteen-months period, and Specialized Agency people hoped that this would grow larger year by year. There even began to be something like competition in courting underdeveloped countries for projects (any Technical Assistance project has to be requested by the country in which it is to be carried out). But the boom in beneficence failed to expand according to expectations. The fund for 1952 was nineteen millions and while it increased in 1953 to twenty-one millions, the Agencies which were allotted shares of it had to come back to earth and concern themselves with the quality of their projects rather than the quantity. Some officials considered this a good thing, though not for publication.

At times the functions of different Specialized Agencies approach so closely that overlapping becomes almost unavoidable. Take the tree example. Its nurture and protection from insects are certainly within the province of the Food and Agriculture Organization. Cutting it down may be, too, and chopping it up for firewood. But if the wood is to be used to make a table or a chair, say, just where does FAO stop before it impinges on International Labour Organisation territory? Or UNESCO's, for that matter, which teaches handicrafts?

Such jurisdictional questions are usually minor, however, and on the whole the Agencies get along well with one another.

What their efforts in the long run will mean to the human race is still too early to judge. Some observers feel that the technological strides of advanced nations in recent times are so great that they have reduced the chances of underdeveloped areas' catching up to an all-time low. As Dr. Laubach complained, the illiterate, the poor and the diseased reproduce faster than the more fortunate part of the human race so far has been able to create literacy, decent jobs and proper health conditions for them.

Nevertheless, the Specialized Agencies are a brave and hopeful new venture. Some, as individual projects (ICAO, for example), are complete innovations. For others, longer established, the worldwide character of their present operations is unprecedented. And, certainly, the co-ordinated work of all of them, on an earth-circling scale, is something that never before has been tried.

The idea of persuading the human race to raise itself economically and culturally by the bootstraps—using the little money available to UN agencies as a kind of advertising fund—may seem over-ambitious to some. But pilot projects in food production, in education, in labor training already have shown far more than promising results. The "Each One Teach One" technique has given a fine starting account of itself. With time it may prove to be the geometrical progression the world needs to solve its desperate human problems.

If the concerted drives of the dozen Specialized Agencies, which deal in one way or another with almost all the peaceful activities and aspirations of mankind, have any large measure of success, one great breeding ground of wars will disappear. It is true that discontent can be whipped up to the fighting pitch in technologically advanced countries like Germany or Japan, and that underdeveloped countries simply cannot wage a modern war. But the colossal inequalities of our world are an invitation to trouble. Whatever the Specialized Agencies do to raise living standards in the less privileged areas is all to the good. And it promises to be a great deal.

CHAPTER 4

The Private Citizen's Part

WHEN ILO's director, Albert Thomas, wrote his indignant letter to Lloyd George in the early days of the League of Nations it was generally considered as something approaching a breach of etiquette, if not worse. His point, the question of labor conditions in the then newly established Soviet regime of Russia, had an undeniable significance. But at that time protocol was more important. The League, when it functioned at all, functioned on a very high level and anyone of less than ambassadorial rank rarely was seen, let alone heard. Albert Thomas' *démarche* made a sensation, but it was definitely not a popularity conquest for him personally. It was through Mr. Roosevelt, Mr. Churchill and some other modern statesmen, much later, that the international importance of Everyman's opinion began to be understood.

The sometimes maligned United States State Department deserves a word of credit in this respect. At the San Francisco conference which wrote the UN Charter the State Department invited representatives of Non-Governmental Organizations to sit in and help. As one result, specific provision was made in the Charter for such private organizations to co-operate practically with the UN. As another direct result, representatives of women's organizations succeeded in getting distaff rights written into the international constitution over the resistance of die-hard masculinists.

Philosophically minded UN people emphasize the point that the Charter's wording starts "We the peoples." Not "We the Governments, the Dictators, Kings, Presidents or what not." "We the

peoples." We the human beings. And the Charter goes on to specify
ways in which private organizations may make themselves felt at
the world's highest political council tables.

It's hard to overemphasize the significance of this fact. Everyone
knows that the YMCA exists, that the International Chamber of
Commerce promotes business, that trade union organizations watch
over labor rights, that child welfare outfits do what they can to protect helpless youngsters. But the day-by-day functioning of such
NGO's in connection with the UN is something that gets far less
attention than it deserves.

UN people say one of the most dramatic examples of a Non-Governmental Organization's work is Tony Sender's exposé of forced
labor. The story is too long to present in detail. And it isn't Tony
Sender's story entirely: without the support of Matthew Woll, her
American Federation of Labor boss, this refugee from the Nazis
never could have forced the facts of Soviet slave labor to international attention. At the European meeting of the Economic and
Social Council in mid-1953, a curtain was drawn over the tragic
story as a political concession to the "new look" regime in the Kremlin, but the horrid details are still in the record.

Another NGO target is the explosive issue of petroleum. No one
in the United States need worry about criticizing Russian labor
policies, but comments on Standard Oil may entail a certain caution. The word "cartel" has unpleasant connotations and it was understandable that the world's biggest oil producers, American, British
and Dutch, opposed publicizing a report on their quiet agreements.
It took enormous effort on the part of Senator Sparkman, aided by
the International Co-operative Alliance, to get the report out
into the open. It seems unlikely that a gallon of gasoline will go
down much in price as a result of the NGO effort, but the fact that
such closely guarded high-level financial operations were disclosed
to the public is impressive. Only a Non-Governmental Organization
would have the intestinal fortitude to bring such a thing to pass.
Only an NGO would have the time, courage and endurance to
keep at it till it did come to pass.

It's estimated that there are thirty million American members of NGO's connected with the UN, and 400 million the world over.

The Economic and Social Council has a Standing Committee devoted to the Non-Governmental Organizations and it depends on them for much of the support of its work, also for much of the work itself. Actually, as time goes on and the relations between the more active NGO's and the Council grow closer, it becomes harder and harder to find the dividing line between the governmentally appointed international workers and the nongovernmentally appointed. Their purposes, of course, are identical, and their means of accomplishing them often overlap.

Counting all the organizations that make any effort, however spasmodic, to keep up with UN activities, there are approximately four thousand listed. The majority of these are national outfits that content themselves with reporting events at the UN to their memberships. There are 239 mostly international organizations that take a more active part in UN affairs. These, upon application to the Secretary-General, have been assigned three forms of status: Category A, Category B and listing on the register. Category A is the highest form of consultative status, authorizing its members to appear before the Economic and Social Council, to present written or oral statements, and to suggest items for the Council's provisional agenda. Category B (and some organizations merely listed on the register) also may present written statements on subjects in which they are deemed to have special competence, but whereas Category A is permitted a comparatively garrulous two thousand words of length, Category B is limited to five hundred words. The Secretary-General may invite organizations on the register to submit written statements. And the Economic and Social Council Committee on Non-Governmental Organizations may at any time call in members of Categories A or B for consultation on matters considered to be within their special competence.

International and national NGO's may ask for the privilege of appointing observers to sit in and report on UN public meetings. These observers have fairly regular background conferences of their own, separate from those of newspaper, radio and press association people, at which they are briefed by the Assistant Secretary-General in charge of the Department of Public Information or another UN official of similar rank. This is an important part of DPI's work, since the UN, always hard-pressed to find money to pay for its necessary activities, depends heavily on NGO's to keep the world public informed of its operations. NGO publications, NGO speakers and NGO writers for non-NGO publications compete with the UN's own vast mill of words to tell what Dorothy Lewis' Radio Department calls "the greatest story being told." This is not the least valuable of NGO functions.

The range of NGO interests and special knowledge is vitally significant to the UN. Some of the items suggested to the Economic and Social Council by NGO's on which ECOSOC took action give an idea of the direction NGO thinking takes:

1. Equal pay for equal work for men and women—World Federation of Trade Unions.

2. Forced labor—American Federation of Labor.

3. Administration of oil resources—International Co-operative Alliance.

4. Abolition of discriminatory measures of an economic and social character from which workers suffer on grounds of race and color—World Federation of Trade Unions.

5. Study of the economic situation of Africa—World Federation of United Nations Associations.

6. Conclusion of an International Convention on Customs Treatment of Samples and Advertising Material—International Chamber of Commerce.

Up to April, 1953, NGO's had submitted 345 written statements to the Economic and Social Council.

There is a phrase sometimes used about NGO work—"a two-way street." One direction of the effort is to help shape UN policy. Often this occurs in the Specialized Agencies. The International Chamber of Commerce, for example, makes studies of economic subjects which are frequently published by the UN. The World Health Organization accepts advice from individual doctors or medical and public health associations. The Food and Agriculture Organization takes heed of farmers.

Most often the policy-affecting work of NGO's is economic or technical. But sometimes it's political, too. The political achievements, however, are rarely quotable, for obvious reasons. If it became known that an NGO rewrote the truce proposal of a UN member nation, both the government that presented the proposal and the NGO would be embarrassed. And the NGO might lose its usefulness.

The other direction of the "two-way street" is spreading the UN gospel. A year or so ago Dorothy Lewis made a strenuous speaking tour, talking chiefly to NGO conventions. The strongest impression she got from it was the effect of association. It made no great difference, she insisted, what she said or how she said it. The impact of the UN idea came not out of her words, but out of the fact that trusted friends and leaders of the audiences shared the platform with her and made anything she said believable and worth hearing. And they asked her to speak at other meetings—hundreds of them. This lending of local authority to UN aims is far more important to the development of the international organization than it might seem.

Lyman White, an astute student of the history of international affairs, emphasizes the novelty of all intergovernmental organizations, pointing out that "at least 90 per cent of the present vast international machinery, governmental and nongovernmental, has been created during the last three decades." Most of the early experiments were nongovernmental, or, like the Universal Postal Union and the International Telecommunication Union, representative of governments but privately operated. The experience in international cooperation acquired by Non-Governmental Organizations through the years and now made constantly available to the UN is not the least of its assets.

Note on the Future

COLERIDGE phrased the old thought: "And in to-day already walks tomorrow." No one is expected to make an acceptable prediction for next year's UN or next year's world. A decade from now is more uncertain, and a generation inconceivable. But we do have today. And despite the all-too-apparent tragedies of our time there are good things on which to base hope for the future.

One good thing that often escapes attention is the fact that we are beginning to know more about ourselves. The UN, as the world's greatest repository of information, is a reflection of the twentieth century. We may not yet have learned how to act sensibly on the facts, but at least they are becoming available.

The UN's facts are mostly technical—economic, financial, scientific, statistical. Political truths are still rare and difficult to prove. But the direction the UN has chosen for its long-term course is surely toward verity. The public availability of its information, the openness of most of its meetings, the constant stress on President Wilson's ideal of open covenants openly arrived at are well-marked highways to ultimate revelation.

There is an assumption of long standing in some quarters of the American press that American diplomats are always outwitted by wily foreigners. This assumption is not shared by foreigners, who point to concrete historical facts like: (1) the Louisiana Purchase, from which we gained the states of Louisiana, Arkansas, Oklahoma, Kansas, Missouri, Nebraska, Iowa, the Dakotas, Montana, most of Minnesota and parts of Colorado and Wyoming for fifteen million dollars; (2) the accession of the Territory of Alaska, which we got from Russia for seven millions; (3) the annexation from Spain of the Philippine Islands, after a war which Congress expressly resolved was declared to free Cuba. Foreigners, recalling such events, do not unduly worry about American diplomats' ability to take care of American interests. They do, however, worry about United States willingness and ability to take care of its responsibilities to the rest of the world.

The American share of total UN expenses, including Technical Assistance and the Specialized Agencies, amounts to about seventy-five cents per capita per year. Although the sum is less than we willingly spend on a single aircraft carrier, we complain about it, chiefly because we pay more than other member nations. If we could accurately foresee a change in the reluctant attitude of so many Americans toward the UN, we might more confidently predict a successful future for the organization.

As Joseph Stalin's imperialistic course of action after World War II threw off all the early logic of the UN, so his death has disorganized current thinking. How the resulting internal political upheaval in Russia will eventually affect the rest of the world is impossible to guess. How much unrest there actually is behind the Iron Curtain and what will come of it, no one can say. How the spectacular native moves toward self-government in the heavily populated territories of Asia and Africa will turn out is another question for the crystal ball. But a point to remember about the UN's role in these matters is that both its thinking and its practical agencies favor land reform—and land reform is the most ancient and powerful of all revolutionary forces. Therefore, though landowners may oppose UN philosophy, the many hundreds of millions of soil-tillers will certainly sympathize.

How the twenty Latin-American member nations will influence the future history of the UN is still another question. Relative national power changes with time and the basis on which UN decisions are made now may be unrecognizable fifty years hence.

What is reasonable to predict is that the UN will continue and become more effective with time. Its present political weaknesses may be partly offset by its economic efforts and the member nations may sometime decide to trust it with the necessary powers to keep the world in order. Meanwhile, the everyday work it does is the best thing that ever has happened to the human race.

101 Questions and Answers About the UN

1. *Q.:* When does the General Assembly meet?
   A.: According to its Rules of Procedure, the General Assembly meets in regular session once a year starting on the third Tuesday of September. However, by agreement of a majority of the members the date of the opening of the session may be postponed.

2. *Q.:* When does the Security Council meet?
   A.: According to the Charter, the Security Council "shall be so organized as to be able to function continuously" meaning that state members of the Security Council have permanent representatives at the headquarters of the United Nations so that they are available for meetings called on quick notice. Meetings are called by the chairman of the Council and according to the Rules of Procedure of the Security Council the interval between the meetings "shall not exceed fourteen days." However, this latter provision is not always followed.

Attendance by Visitors

3. *Q.:* How can visitors get tickets?
   A.: By calling the admissions office at UN Headquarters at 8:30 A.M. or later the day of a meeting or the day before.

4. *Q.:* Are visitors allowed in all the meetings?

151

A.: Visitors are allowed in all public meetings, space permitting.

5. Q.: What is a "closed" meeting?

A.: A closed meeting is one to which only members and their advisers are permitted.

6. Q.: Why is a meeting canceled?

A.: A meeting is canceled by the chairman at the request of a member if the reason for the request is deemed sufficiently important.

Mechanics of Meetings

7. Q.: Are meetings recorded? Why is there duplication of recordings and verbatim reports?

A.: All of the meetings are voice-recorded by UN Radio for the archives. Verbatim reports are also made because these can be easily duplicated for the members and Secretariat. In case of question, the verbatim record can be checked with the record of the meeting.

8. Q.: How do the earphones work?

A.: There is a dial with numbers 1, 2, 3, 4, 5, and 6, to cover the five official languages of the UN, plus the direct transmission of the speaker's voice. The listener can "tune in" by turning the dial to whatever language he wants— Chinese, French, English, Spanish, Russian or the original.

9. Q.: What is a Rapporteur?

A.: A Rapporteur, or reporter, is responsible for drawing up the official report of a meeting or session.

10. Q.: How many people participate in a meeting?

A.: Representation varies according to the Charter-dictated size of the body. As for actual "participation," this depends upon how many delegates wish to be heard on a certain item.

11. Q.: May visitors take pictures?

A.: Yes, if it can be done without interfering with the conduct of UN business.

12. *Q.:* Where does the chairman of a committee sit?

   A.: The chairman sits in the middle of the long table facing the other members.

13. *Q.:* What are the Rules of Procedure?

   A.: The General Assembly and the Security Council, Trusteeship Council and Economic and Social Council all determine their own parliamentary rules. Voting varies from a simple majority decision to the veto right owned by permanent members of the Security Council.

14. *Q.:* There are sixty flags—what is the sixtieth to join the UN family?

   A.: Indonesia.

15. *Q.:* What is the story of the UN flag?

   A.: The UN emblem was designed by the Presentation Branch of the U.S. Office of Strategic Services in April, 1945, in response to a request for a button to be worn by delegates to the San Francisco Conference. The San Francisco design was a circular representation of a map of the world, extending to 40th Parallel South, and with 100th Meridian West of Greenwich in the lower vertical position. The Secretary-General urged the adoption of an official seal and emblem of the UN and on December 7, 1946, the General Assembly approved with slight modification the San Francisco design. The revised emblem consisted of a map of the world on a pole aximental by equidistant projection, sided by two olive branches, ancient Greek symbols of peace. On October 20, 1947, the Assembly adopted without objection a resolution that the flag of the UN should be the official emblem adopted by the General Assembly. The UN flag may on no account be displayed lower than the flag of any individual nation, nor be smaller. The UN flag may be displayed on either side of any other flag without being deemed to be subordinated. The UN flag is flown in all Trust Territories alongside the flag of the Administering Authority.

16. *Q.:* Are all the UN meetings broadcast?
    A.: No. Only those of particular interest.
17. *Q.:* In what languages are they broadcast?
    A.: UN broadcasts often are rebroadcast by member nations; therefore there is no way to tell the number of languages used.

Interpretation System

18. *Q.:* What are the five official languages?
    A.: Chinese, French, English, Spanish and Russian.
19. *Q.:* Why is French used in the signs around UN Headquarters?
    A.: Although there are five official languages, French and English, as the most common tongues of diplomacy, have been the "working" languages. Spanish is to be added.
20. *Q.:* What are the language requirements for an interpreter?
    A.: The average interpreter must know two languages, say French and Spanish, well enough to translate both into colloquial English. However, Chinese interpreters need only be able to translate Chinese into English and English into Chinese.
21. *Q.:* How does simultaneous interpretation work?
    A.: The interpreters listen to the speech in one language with earphones and interpret it into other languages on their microphones. The audience as well as the delegates "tune in" to whatever language they wish to hear.
22. *Q.:* How much do interpreters make?
    A.: About $100 to $200 per week.
23. *Q.:* How can a person train himself to become an interpreter?
    A.: UN personnel wish they knew the answer to this question. A competent interpreter is very hard to find, and practically impossible to train.
24. *Q.:* Spain is not a member of the United Nations. Why is Spanish an official language?
    A.: Spanish is an official language because of the twenty Latin American member countries where Spanish is spoken—also the Philippines.

25. Q.: Will Chinese last as an official language if the Communists are seated?

A.: Yes. The seating of the delegates of the People's Republic of China in place of the Nationalist Government delegates would not change the status of Chinese as an official language.

26. Q.: How do the interpreters manage when a slang expression is used?

A.: The interpreters are supposed to be sufficiently fluent so that they can use a similar slang expression in the language into which they are interpreting the speech.

Budget

27. Q.: What does the budget include?

A.: The budget includes all of the expenses of the United Nations, its various bodies, offices, missions, etc.

28. Q.: What is the largest part spent for?

A.: For salaries and maintenance of UN Headquarters in New York.

29. Q.: Who pays for the budget?

A.: The state members of the United Nations.

30. Q.: What determines how large the budget shall be and how much each country pays?

A.: The Secretary-General draws up a tentative budget based upon the budget of the year before and expected expenditures for the next year. This is examined and revised if necessary by the Advisory Committee on Administrative and Budgetary Questions. The Committee on Contributions determines what percentage of the budget each member should pay. The budget and scale of contributions are then discussed in Committee 5 of the General Assembly and finally adopted by the General Assembly.

31. Q.: Is membership in any of the councils determined by the amount of contribution to the budget?

A.: No.

32. *Q.:* Is there an article limiting the contribution of any one country to one-third of the entire budget?

   A.: Yes. In 1952 the General Assembly adopted a resolution stating that no country should contribute more than one-third of the budget of the UN.

33. *Q.:* Who pays the delegates?

   A.: The United Nations pays for the travel of five representatives from each member state to meetings of the General Assembly, travel and subsistence for members of special committees and commissions (sometimes only travel), and travel and subsistence for members of regional commissions. As a rule no provision is made for members of the Security Council, ECOSOC and the Trusteeship Council on the theory that these meetings are generally held at Headquarters.

   All other expenses, including salaries, are paid by the member states.

34. *Q.:* By whom are the personnel of the UN paid?

   A.: The personnel of the UN are paid out of the general budget of the UN, regardless of nationality of the employee.

35. *Q.:* Why is the U.S. the largest contributor to the UN budget?

   A.: The contribution of each member state of the UN is determined on the ability to pay.

36. *Q.:* Is it because the United States has the largest delegation?

   A.: No, this has nothing to do with the scale of contributions.

37. *Q.:* Why is the U.S.S.R. share of the budget so small?

   A.: The U.S.S.R. contribution, like that of the other members, is determined by the Committee on Contributions and finally adopted by the General Assembly, on the basis of ability to pay. The U.S.S.R. contribution has been raised during recent years.

38. *Q.:* What happens if a government changes hands and has paid part of its contribution? Does the new government pay the rest?

   A.: Yes, the new government is obligated to pay the remainder of the contribution.

Structure and Organization of the UN
General Organization and Charter

39. *Q.:* What determines whether or not a nation will be admitted to the UN?

    A.: According to the Charter, membership is open to all "peace-loving states which accept the obligations contained in the present Charter, and in the judgment of the Organization, are able and willing to carry out these obligations." Membership is effected by a decision of the General Assembly upon the recommendation of the Security Council.

40. *Q.:* If a country gives up its membership in the UN, can it return?

    A.: In the Charter no provision is made for withdrawing or returning, but presumably both are possible.

41. *Q.:* Are there any provisions for barring a nation from the UN?

    A.: See Answer 39. According to the Charter a nation may be expelled by vote of the General Assembly upon recommendation of the Security Council.

42. *Q.:* Does the General Assembly have to approve any decision made in councils and committees?

    A.: The General Assembly receives reports from all bodies of of the UN and can make recommendations to any one of them. Individual decisions of the councils and committees are not necessarily subject to approval of the General Assembly except in cases where expenditure of money is involved, or adherence by member states is called for (as in the Genocide Convention), etc.

43. *Q.:* What is UNESCO?

    A.: The United Nations Educational, Scientific and Cultural Organization is one of the Specialized Agencies of the United Nations.

44. *Q.:* How is an organization like UNICEF created. What is its status with regard to the machinery of the UN?

A.: The United Nations International Children's Fund was established by vote of the General Assembly in December, 1946. It is not a Specialized Agency, but an integral part of the United Nations. Its Executive Board was named by the General Assembly in the resolution establishing the Fund.

Security Council

45. *Q.:* What problems does the Security Council discuss?

A.: Any matter relating to the maintenance of peace and security brought to its attention by a member of the United Nations, by the Secretary-General or by a nonmember, party to a dispute, which agrees in advance to accept the obligations of the Charter.

46. *Q.:* How may a nation not a member of the UN bring a dispute before the Security Council?

A.: By accepting in advance, "for the purposes of the dispute, the obligations of pacific settlement provided in the present Charter."

47. *Q.:* Why does the Security Council change chairmen each month?

A.: Since the Security Council is so organized as to be in continuous session, the Rules of Procedure provide that the chairmanship of the Council be changed in rotation each month (in the English alphabetical order) so that all members will have equal opportunities.

48. *Q.:* How many nations are permanent in the Security Council? Why are they permanent members? How decided?

A.: There are five permanent members in the Security Council: China, France, the United Kingdom, the United States and the U.S.S.R. These are specified in the Charter. They were designated as permanent members at the time the Charter was drafted on the theory that on questions regarding the maintenance of peace and security, the so-called Big Five, who would have the primary responsibility for the maintenance of peace, should always have a voice.

Trusteeship

49. *Q.*: What does Trusteeship mean?

  A.: Trusteeship is the term used to define the relationship between an administering power and non-self-governing territories designated as "trust" areas.

50. *Q.*: What is the Trusteeship Council? How does it operate?

  A.: The Trusteeship Council is composed of the nations administering trust areas, the permanent members of the Security Council that are not Administering Authorities of such trust areas and as many nations without trust areas as necessary to make an equal division between administering and nonadministering powers. The Trusteeship Council examines and makes recommendations concerning the administration of the trust areas; it receives petitions from the inhabitants of the areas and sends visiting missions to the areas to make on-the-spot investigations.

51. *Q.*: What can the UN do if an Administering Authority violates its treaty with the UN?

  A.: The Trusteeship Council can censure the Administering Authority, send visiting missions, etc., and make recommendations for rectifying the action. The General Assembly could also make recommendations.

  The UN has no authority to "make" the territory independent, but the General Assembly has asked each Administering Authority to indicate "the period of time in which it is expected that the Trust Territory shall attain the objective of self-government or independence."

52. *Q.*: What is a U.S. Trust Territory?

  A.: There is the Trust Territory of the Pacific Islands (the Marianas, Marshalls and Carolines) under U.S. administration, which is a "strategic area trusteeship." The agreement under which this last area is administered was approved by the Security Council rather than by the General Assembly.

International Court

53. *Q.:* How are the judges appointed? By whom?

A.: The fifteen judges of the Court are elected for nine-year terms by the General Assembly and the Security Council, voting independently. No two may be nationals of the same state. Nominations are sent in by the member states.

54. *Q.:* Where does the Court meet?

A.: At The Hague, Netherlands.

55. *Q.:* How is the Court organized?

A.: The Court elects a President and Vice President for three-year terms, a Registrar and such other officers as may be necessary. The full Court sits except when it decides to form a "chamber" of three or more judges to consider certain types of cases.

56. *Q.:* Has the Court taken any important decisions? Done any important work?

A.: The Court has had several important cases brought to it and has rendered important decisions and advisory opinions on the Corfu Channel Case, the Anglo-Iranian Oil Case, rights of U.S. nationals in Morocco, admission of members to the UN, reparations to UN personnel for injuries suffered in the service of the UN, etc. Perhaps one of the most far-reaching was the advisory opinion in the last-named case which declared that the UN had an international personality and was able to sue for reparations from a member or nonmember state.

Secretariat

57. *Q.:* How long does the same personnel represent their country in the Secretariat?

A.: The members of the Secretariat are selected on as wide a geographical basis as possible, but no member "represents" the country of his nationality. Tenure of office is decided according to regulations approved by the General Assembly. Members are retired at the age of sixty.

58. Q.: Does a Secretariat employee cease to be a citizen of his own country?

A.: No, but he takes an oath giving his primary allegiance to the international organization and guaranteeing that he will not be swayed in his work for the UN by any national or partisan considerations.

59. Q.: Does he pay taxes?

A.: All UN employees except U.S. nationals are exempt by their governments from income taxes. Other than relief from income taxes, UN employees enjoy very few diplomatic immunities or privileges.

60. Q.: What does the Secretary-General preside over? What is his job, his responsibility? By whom is he appointed?

A.: The Secretary-General is the chief administrative officer of the United Nations. He does not "preside" over anything. He performs the chief administrative functions of the UN, makes an annual report to the General Assembly on the work of the UN during the preceding year, appoints the staff of the UN, and may bring to the attention of the Security Council or General Assembly any matter he thinks may threaten the maintenance of international peace and security. The Secretary-General is appointed by the General Assembly on recommendation of the Security Council.

61. Q.: Is there a representative of the Secretary-General at all meetings?

A.: Yes.

Voting

62. Q.: What majority is needed to pass a resolution?

A.: This varies from body to body. Resolutions are adopted in the General Assembly by a two-thirds majority of members present and voting, if the question is an important one, or by a simple majority if the question is of a more routine nature. Committees of the Assembly take decisions by a simple majority.

In the Security Council decisions are taken by a majority of seven, including the affirmative votes of the permanent members. Procedural questions are decided by the affirmative votes of any seven members.

Resolutions in the Economic and Social Council are adopted by a majority of the members present and voting. The same is true in the Trusteeship Council.

Commissions and committees take decisions by simple majority.

63. Q.: What is meant by abstention?

A.: Abstention means that a member does not vote either for or against a resolution.

64. Q.: What happens to the unanimous vote of the five permanent members in the Security Council on substantive matters when Russia is not present?

A.: During the time the Soviet Union was absent from the Security Council, the Council took the position that an absence was tantamount to an abstention. The Soviet Union itself initiated the custom that an abstention is not a veto. It must also be remembered that the Charter says that the vote must include the "concurring votes of the permanent members"; it does not specify "all" or "five."

Membership on Councils and Committees

65. Q.: How are countries appointed to councils and commissions?

A.: The General Assembly elects the members of the councils and any commission or committee it might establish.

The councils elect the members of any commissions or committees they might establish.

66. Q.: Is geographical distribution the same on all the committees, commissions and councils?

A.: An effort is always made to have as wide a geographical

distribution as possible; however, membership on the various councils, committees and commissions is not the same.

67. *Q.:* Are the "Big Five" on all the councils?

   A.: According to the Charter provisions, the "Big Five" are automatically members of the Security Council and the Trusteeship Council. It is not mandatory that they be members of the Economic and Social Council, but they have been so far.

68. *Q.:* Is there any body where all the nations are represented?

   A.: All nations are represented in the General Assembly and in the six main committees of the General Assembly.

Substance Questions Regarding Enforcement:

69. *Q.:* What force is there behind the UN now?

   A.: At the present time the UN has the force of world public opinion.

70. *Q.:* Why doesn't the UN have an army? Isn't there Charter provision for one?

   A.: The agreements envisioned under Articles 43 and 45 of the Charter have not been completed, primarily due to tensions existing among the Big Five and lack of agreement on the Military Staff Committee which is composed of the Big Five. The Collective Measures Committee, however, established by the Assembly's "Uniting for Peace" Resolution in 1950, is studying measures for collective security, including a UN legion. Also, member countries have been asked to indicate what forces they would be willing to contribute for future UN action.

71. *Q.:* Can the UN do anything when one country is sending another armaments and causing a threat to the peace? If so, what?

   A.: The UN cannot prevent one country from sending armaments into another country. Such an act does not necessarily cause a threat to the peace of the world; in fact it might help to build up the forces of collective security.

Miscellaneous

72. *Q.:* What nations have applied for membership in the UN and not been admitted?

A.: Albania, Mongolian People's Republic, Jordan, Ireland, Portugal, Hungary, Italy, Austria, Rumania, Bulgaria, Finland, Ceylon, Republic of Korea, Democratic People's Republic of Korea, Nepal, Vietnam, Libya, Democratic People's Vietnam, Cambodia, Japan, Laos.

73. *Q.:* What about the membership of Spain?

A.: By resolution of the General Assembly in 1946 Spain was barred from membership in the UN and the Specialized Agencies. In 1950, however, the General Assembly reconsidered the question and decided that the Specialized Agencies should be free to decide for themselves whether Spain should become a member and be allowed to participate in their work. Spain now is a member of several UN Specialized Services.

74. *Q.:* Is the Point Four Program a U.S. or a UN program? What is the difference?

A.: Point Four is the name given to the United States bilateral program of technical assistance. The UN Technical Assistance Program is a multilateral one in which all members of the United Nations are invited to participate.

75. *Q.:* What per cent of the world's people are represented in the UN?

A.: Over 1,800,000,000 people are now represented in the United Nations—something like 80 per cent of the world's population.

76. *Q.:* Do the families of the Secretariat live in the building?

A.: No. The Secretariat Building contains the working offices of the various departments under the administration of the Secretary-General, plus liaison offices of the Specialized Agencies, newspaper and radio rooms and space for miscellaneous purposes. None of the sixty member nations has office space in the Secretariat Building.

77. *Q.:* Is there a UN coin?

    A.: No.

78. *Q.:* Does the UN profit from sales of UN stamps?

    A.: Not from those used for mailing; only from those sold to philatelists.

79. *Q.:* Has the UN budget increased or decreased since the organization started?

    A.: The normal budget for 1953 was less than the one for 1952. Funds for the Specialized Agencies, however, and for the Expanded Technical Assistance Program are not included in the normal UN budget. The total of all three comes to less than $100,000,000 a year.

80. *Q.:* Who would be responsible in the event of a crime committed on UN property?

    A.: Depending on the nature of the offense: municipal, state or Federal authorities would be in charge, unless special legislation of the UN conflicted with the American statute, in which case UN regulations would take precedence. Normal procedure would be for UN guards to apprehend the transgressor and turn him over to the American authorities.

81. *Q.:* How could the Korean conflict be a UN operation, with Russia a member of the international organization?

    A.: The UN forces resisting aggression in Korea were fighting only against Northern Korean and Chinese Communist armies. No question of Soviet Russia's connection with the conflict was formally raised.

82. *Q.:* Does the Meditation Room have any special symbol?

    A.: No, except for its lack of symbols. The design is intended to make all religious creeds comfortable.

83. *Q.:* How many vetoes have been registered?

    A.: 55 by Russia; one by France; one by France and Russia.

84. *Q.:* Is it possible to revise the UN Charter?

    A.: Yes. One of its provisions requires that it automatically receive reconsideration after the first ten years. Otherwise, a two-thirds majority of the General Assembly is necessary for any specific change, with ratification by two-thirds of the UN members, including all permanent members of the Security Council.

85. *Q.:* Did anyone besides Mr. Rockefeller donate the land on which UN Headquarters stands?

   A.: Yes, New York City.

86. *Q.:* Can anyone besides UN employees park his car in the UN garage?

   A.: Yes, people visiting the UN on business.

87. *Q.:* Are there eating facilities for visitors not on UN business?
   A.: No.

88. *Q.:* Is the UN playground restricted to children of UN employees?

   A.: No, any child may play there. A UN guard supervises the playground.

89. *Q.:* What can I do to entertain UN personnel?

   A.: Telephone PLaza 4-1234, Ext. 3361, or write Miss Aroos Benneyan of Volunteer Services, United Nations, New York.

90. *Q.:* Can I, as an individual, make a monetary contribution to the UN?

   A.: Yes, there is a general fund. Write to the Secretary-General, United Nations, New York.

91. *Q.:* How can I keep up with UN activities?

   A.: You can subscribe to the *United Nations Reporter* (published monthly), subscription price, $1 per year; or to the *Bulletin* (published biweekly), subscription price, $4.50 per year.

92. *Q.:* Can a private citizen contribute to the UN Library?

   A.: Yes, exchange services are always welcome. Any documents from however remote a source are received with gratitude by the UN Library.

93. *Q.:* How can I get someone to speak about the UN for my local organization?

A.: Write Volunteer Speakers, Department of Public Information, United Nations, New York, or telephone PLaza 4-1234, Ext. 3411.

94. Q.: How do you pronounce the name of the new Secretary-General, Dag Hammarskjold?

A.: Mr. Hammarskjold has publicly announced that he does not mind having his name pronounced "Hammer-shield," since this is the meaning of the word in English and no average American could get close to the proper pronunciation.

95. Q.: What is the oldest organization connected with the UN?

A.: International Telecommunication Union.

96. Q.: What are the three Specialized Agencies that Soviet Russia still supports and co-operates with?

A.: World Meteorological Organization, Universal Postal Union and International Telecommunication Union.

97. Q.: Where was the first meeting of the UN held?

A.: In London, England.

98. Q.: How long does the Secretary-General serve? The President of the General Assembly?

A.: By resolution of the General Assembly the Secretary-General serves a five-year term and is eligible for reappointment; the President of the Assembly, under the Charter, for the duration of one session.

99. Q.: Why is the no-smoking rule in the elevators so rigidly observed?

A.: Because some UN personnel have religious objections to the use of tobacco.

100. Q.: Are there pages, as in the United States Senate?

A.: No. There are messengers who deliver mail, but the chief dependence for communication is on the telephone.

101. Q.: How long does it take to wash the UN Headquarters windows?

A.: A crew of nine men works the year around keeping the 6,800 windows polished.

Charter of the United Nations and Statute of the International Court of Justice

CHARTER OF THE UNITED NATIONS

WE THE PEOPLES OF THE UNITED NATIONS DETERMINED to save succeeding generations from the scourge of war, which twice in our lifetime has brought untold sorrow to mankind, and

to reaffirm faith in fundamental human rights, in the dignity and worth of the human person, in the equal rights of men and women and of nations large and small, and

to establish conditions under which justice and respect for the obligations arising from treaties and other sources of international law can be maintained, and

to promote social progress and better standards of life in larger freedom,

AND FOR THESE ENDS to practice tolerance and live together in peace with one another as good neighbors, and

to unite our strength to maintain international peace and security, and to ensure, by the acceptance of principles and the institution of methods, that armed force shall not be used, save in the common interest, and

to employ international machinery for the promotion of the economic and social advancement of all peoples,

HAVE RESOLVED TO COMBINE OUR EFFORTS TO ACCOMPLISH THESE AIMS. Accordingly, our respective Governments, through representatives assembled in the city of San Francisco, who have exhibited their full powers found to be in good and due form, have agreed to the present Charter of the United Nations and do hereby establish an international organization to be known as the United Nations.

Chapter I

PURPOSES AND PRINCIPLES

Article 1

The Purposes of the United Nations are:

1. To maintain international peace and security, and to that end: to take effective collective measures for the prevention and removal of threats to the peace, and for the suppression of acts of aggression or other breaches of the peace, and to bring about by peaceful means, and in conformity with the principles of justice and international law, adjustment or settlement of international disputes or situations which might lead to a breach of the peace;

2. To develop friendly relations among nations based on respect for the principle of equal rights and self-determination of peoples, and to take other appropriate measures to strengthen universal peace;

3. To achieve international cooperation in solving international problems of an economic, social, cultural, or humanitarian character, and in promoting and encouraging respect for human rights and for fundamental freedoms for all without distinction as to race, sex, language, or religion; and

4. To be a center for harmonizing the actions of nations in the attainment of these common ends.

Article 2

The Organization and its Members, in pursuit of the Purposes stated in Article 1, shall act in accordance with the following Principles.

1. The Organization is based on the principle of the sovereign equality of all its Members.

2. All Members, in order to ensure to all of them the rights and benefits resulting from membership, shall fulfil in good faith the obligations assumed by them in accordance with the present Charter.

3. All Members shall settle their international disputes by peaceful means in such a manner that international peace and security, and justice, are not endangered.

4. All Members shall refrain in their international relations from the threat or use of force against the territorial integrity or political independence of any state, or in any other manner inconsistent with the Purposes of the United Nations.

5. All Members shall give the United Nations every assistance in any action it takes in accordance with the present Charter, and shall refrain from giving assistance to any state against which the United Nations is taking preventive or enforcement action.

6. The Organization shall ensure that states which are not Members of the United Nations act in accordance with these Principles so far as may be necessary for the maintenance of international peace and security.

7. Nothing contained in the present Charter shall authorize the United Nations to intervene in matters which are essentially within the domestic jurisdiction of any state or shall require the Members to submit such matters to settlement under the present Charter; but this principle shall not prejudice the application of enforcement measures under Chapter VII.

Chapter II

MEMBERSHIP

Article 3

The original Members of the United Nations shall be the states which, having participated in the United Nations Conference on International Organization at San Francisco, or having previously signed the Declaration by United Nations of January 1, 1942, sign the present Charter and ratify it in accordance with Article 110.

Article 4

1. Membership in the United Nations is open to all other peace-loving states which accept the obligations contained in the present Charter and, in the judgment of the Organization, are able and willing to carry out these obligations.

2. The admission of any such state to membership in the United Nations will be effected by a decision of the General Assembly upon the recommendation of the Security Council.

Article 5

A Member of the United Nations against which preventive or enforcement action has been taken by the Security Council may be suspended from the exercise of the rights and privileges of membership by the General Assembly upon the recommendation of the Security Council. The exercise of these rights and privileges may be restored by the Security Council.

Article 6

A Member of the United Nations which has persistently violated the Principles contained in the present Charter may be expelled from the Organization by the General Assembly upon the recommendation of the Security Council.

Chapter III

ORGANS

Article 7

1. There are established as the principal organs of the United Nations: a General Assembly, a Security Council, an Economic and Social Council, a Trusteeship Council, an International Court of Justice, and a Secretariat.

2. Such subsidiary organs as may be found necessary may be established in accordance with the present Charter.

Article 8

The United Nations shall place no restrictions on the eligibility of men and women to participate in any capacity and under conditions of equality in its principal and subsidiary organs.

Chapter IV

THE GENERAL ASSEMBLY

Composition

Article 9

1. The General Assembly shall consist of all the Members of the United Nations.

2. Each Member shall have not more than five representatives in the General Assembly.

Functions and Powers

Article 10

The General Assembly may discuss any questions or any matters within the scope of the present Charter or relating to the powers and functions of any organs provided for in the present Charter, and, except as provided in Article 12, may make recommendations to the Members of the United Nations or to the Security Council or to both on any such questions or matters.

Article 11

1. The General Assembly may consider the general principles of cooperation in the maintenance of international peace and security, including the principles governing disarmament and the regulation of armaments, and may make recommendations with regard to such principles to the Members or to the Security Council or to both.

2. The General Assembly may discuss any questions relating to the maintenance of international peace and security brought before it by any Member of the United Nations, or by the Security Council, or by a state which is not a Member of the United Nations in accordance with Article 35, paragraph 2, and, except as provided in Article 12, may make recommendations with regard to any such question to the state or states concerned or to the Security Council or to both. Any such question on which action is necessary shall be referred to the Security Council by the General Assembly either before or after discussion.

3. The General Assembly may call the attention of the Security Council to situations which are likely to endanger international peace and security.

4. The powers of the General Assembly set forth in this Article shall not limit the general scope of Article 10.

Article 12

1. While the Security Council is exercising in respect of any dispute or situation the functions assigned to it in the present Charter, the General Assembly shall not make any recommendation with regard to that dispute or situation unless the Security Council so requests.

2. The Secretary-General, with the consent of the Security Council, shall notify the General Assembly at each session of any matters relative to the maintenance of international peace and security which are being dealt with by the Security Council and shall similarly notify the Gen-

eral Assembly, or the Members of the United Nations if the General Assembly is not in session, immediately the Security Council ceases to deal with such matters.

Article 13

1. The General Assembly shall initiate studies and make recommendations for the purpose of:

a. promoting international cooperation in the political field and encouraging the progressive development of international law and its codification;

b. promoting international cooperation in the economic, social, cultural, educational, and health fields, and assisting in the realization of human rights and fundamental freedoms for all without distinction as to race, sex, language, or religion.

2. The further responsibilities, functions and powers of the General Assembly with respect to matters mentioned in paragraph 1 b above are set forth in Chapter IX and X.

Article 14

Subject to the provisions of Article 12, the General Assembly may recommend measures for the peaceful adjustment of any situation, regardless of origin, which it deems likely to impair the general welfare or friendly relations among nations, including situations resulting from a violation of the provisions of the present Charter setting forth the Purposes and Principles of the United Nations.

Article 15

1. The General Assembly shall receive and consider annual and special reports from the Security Council; these reports shall include an account of the measures that the Security Council has decided upon or taken to maintain international peace and security.

2. The General Assembly shall receive and consider reports from the other organs of the United Nations.

Article 16

The General Assembly shall perform such functions with respect to the international trusteeship system as are assigned to it under Chapters XII and XIII, including the approval of the trusteeship agreements for areas not designated as strategic.

Article 17

1. The General Assembly shall consider and approve the budget of the Organization.

2. The expenses of the Organization shall be borne by the Members as apportioned by the General Assembly.

3. The General Assembly shall consider and approve any financial and budgetary arrangements with specialized agencies referred to in Article 57 and shall examine the administrative budgets of such specialized agencies with a view to making recommendations to the agencies concerned.

Voting

Article 18

1. Each member of the General Assembly shall have one vote.

2. Decisions of the General Assembly on important questions shall be made by a two-thirds majority of the members present and voting. These questions shall include: recommendations with respect to the maintenance of international peace and security, the election of the non-permanent members of the Security Council, the election of the members of the Economic and Social Council, the election of members of the Trusteeship Council in accordance with paragraph 1 c of Article 86, the admission of new Members to the United Nations, the suspension of the rights and privileges of membership, the expulsion of Members, questions relating to the operation of the trusteeship system, and budgetary questions.

3. Decisions on other questions, including the determination of additional categories of questions to be decided by a two-thirds majority, shall be made by a majority of the members present and voting.

Article 19

A Member of the United Nations which is in arrears in the payment of its financial contributions to the Organization shall have no vote in the General Assembly if the amount of its arrears equals or exceeds the amount of the contributions due from it for the preceding two full years. The General Assembly may, nevertheless, permit such a Member to vote if it is satisfied that the failure to pay is due to conditions beyond the control of the Member.

Procedure

Article 20

The General Assembly shall meet in regular annual sessions and in such special sessions as occasion may require. Special sessions shall be convoked by the Secretary-General at the request of the Security Council or of a majority of the Members of the United Nations.

Article 21

The General Assembly shall adopt its own rules of procedure. It shall elect its President for each session.

Article 22

The General Assembly may establish such subsidiary organs as it deems necessary for the performance of its functions.

Chapter V

THE SECURITY COUNCIL

Composition

Article 23

1. The Security Council shall consist of eleven Members of the United Nations. The Republic of China, France, the Union of Soviet Socialist Republics, the United Kingdom of Great Britain and Northern Ireland, and the United States of America shall be permanent members of the Security Council. The General Assembly shall elect six other Members of the United Nations to be non-permanent members of the Security Council, due regard being specially paid, in the first instance to the contribution of Members of the United Nations to the maintenance of international peace and security and to the other purposes of the Organization, and also to equitable geographical distribution.

2. The non-permanent members of the Security Council shall be elected for a term of two years. In the first election of the non-permanent members, however, three shall be chosen for a term of one year. A retiring member shall not be eligible for immediate re-election.

3. Each member of the Security Council shall have one representative.

Functions and Powers

Article 24

1. In order to ensure prompt and effective action by the United Nations, its Members confer on the Security Council primary responsi-

bility for the maintenance of international peace and security, and agree that in carrying out its duties under this responsibility the Security Council acts on their behalf.

2. In discharging these duties the Security Council shall act in accordance with the Purposes and Principles of the United Nations. The specific powers granted to the Security Council for the discharge of these duties are laid down in Chapters VI, VII, VIII, and XII.

3. The Security Council shall submit annual and, when necessary, special reports to the General Assembly for its consideration.

Article 25

The Members of the United Nations agree to accept and carry out the decisions of the Security Council in accordance with the present Charter.

Article 26

In order to promote the establishment and maintenance of international peace and security with the least diversion for armaments of the world's human and economic resources, the Security Council shall be responsible for formulating, with the assistance of the Military Staff Committee referred to in Article 47, plans to be submitted to the Members of the United Nations for the establishment of a system for the regulation of armaments.

Voting

Article 27

1. Each member of the Security Council shall have one vote.

2. Decisions of the Security Council on procedural matters shall be made by an affirmative vote of seven members.

3. Decisions of the Security Council on all other matters shall be made by an affirmative vote of seven members including the concurring votes of the permanent members; provided that, in decisions under Chapter VI, and under paragraph 3 of Article 52, a party to a dispute shall abstain from voting.

Procedure

Article 28

1. The Security Council shall be so organized as to be able to function continuously. Each member of the Security Council shall for this purpose be represented at all times at the seat of the Organization.

2. The Security Council shall hold periodic meetings at which each of its members may, if it so desires, be represented by a member of the government or by some other specially designated representative.

3. The Security Council may hold meetings at such places other than the seat of the Organization as in its judgment will best facilitate its work.

Article 29

The Security Council may establish such subsidiary organs as it deems necessary for the performance of its functions.

Article 30

The Security Council shall adopt its own rules of procedure, including the method of selecting its President.

Article 31

Any Member of the United Nations which is not a member of the Security Council may participate, without vote, in the discussion of any question brought before the Security Council whenever the latter considers that the interests of that Member are specially affected.

Article 32

Any Member of the United Nations which is not a member of the Security Council or any state which is not a Member of the United Nations, if it is a party to a dispute under consideration by the Security Council, shall be invited to participate, without vote, in the discussion relating to the dispute. The Security Council shall lay down such conditions as it deems just for the participation of a state which is not a Member of the United Nations.

Chapter VI

PACIFIC SETTLEMENT OF DISPUTES

Article 33

1. The parties to any dispute, the continuance of which is likely to endanger the maintenance of international peace and security, shall, first of all, seek a solution by negotiation, enquiry, mediation, conciliation, arbitration, judicial settlement, resort to regional agencies or arrangements, or other peaceful means of their own choice.

2. The Security Council shall, when it deems necessary, call upon the parties to settle their dispute by such means.

Article 34

The Security Council may investigate any dispute, or any situation which might lead to international friction or give rise to a dispute, in order to determine whether the continuance of the dispute or situation is likely to endanger the maintenance of international peace and security.

Article 35

1. Any member of the United Nations may bring any dispute, or any situation of the nature referred to in Article 34, to the attention of the Security Council or of the General Assembly.

2. A state which is not a Member of the United Nations may bring to the attention of the Security Council or of the General Assembly any dispute to which it is a party if it accepts in advance, for the purposes of the dispute, the obligations of pacific settlement provided in the present Charter.

3. The proceedings of the General Assembly in respect of matters brought to its attention under this Article will be subject to the provisions of Articles 11 and 12.

Article 36

1. The Security Council may, at any stage of a dispute of the nature referred to in Article 33 or of a situation of like nature, recommend appropriate procedures or methods of adjustment.

2. The Security Council should take into consideration any procedures for the settlement of the dispute which have already been adopted by the parties.

3. In making recommendations under this Article the Security Council should also take into consideration that legal disputes should as a general rule be referred by the parties to the International Court of Justice in accordance with the provisions of the Statute of the Court.

Article 37

1. Should the parties to a dispute of the nature referred to in Article 33 fail to settle it by the means indicated in that Article, they shall refer it to the Security Council.

2. If the Security Council deems that the continuance of the dispute is in fact likely to endanger the maintenance of international peace and security, it shall decide whether to take action under Article 36 or to recommend such terms of settlement as it may consider appropriate.

Article 38

Without prejudice to the provisions of Articles 33 to 37, the Security Council may, if all the parties to any dispute so request, make recommendations to the parties with a view to a pacific settlement of the dispute.

Chapter VII

ACTION WITH RESPECT TO THREATS TO THE PEACE, BREACHES OF THE PEACE, AND ACTS OF AGGRESSION

Article 39

The Security Council shall determine the existence of any threat to the peace, breach of the peace, or act of aggression and shall make recommendations, or decide what measures shall be taken in accordance with Articles 41 and 42, to maintain or restore international peace and security.

Article 40

In order to prevent an aggravation of the situation, the Security Council may, before making the recommendations or deciding upon the measures provided for in Article 39, call upon the parties concerned to comply with such provisional measures as it deems necessary or desirable. Such provisional measures shall be without prejudice to the rights, claims, or position of the parties concerned. The Security Council shall duly take account of failure to comply with such provisional measures.

Article 41

The Security Council may decide what measures not involving the use of armed force are to be employed to give effect to its decisions, and it may call upon the Members of the United Nations to apply such measures. These may include complete or partial interruption of economic relations and of rail, sea, air, postal, telegraphic, radio, and other means of communication, and the severance of diplomatic relations.

Article 42

Should the Security Council consider that measures provided for in Article 41 would be inadequate or have proved to be inadequate, it may take such action by air, sea, or land forces as may be necessary to maintain or restore international peace and security. Such action may include demonstrations, blockade, and other operations by air, sea, or land forces of Members of the United Nations.

Article 43

1. All Members of the United Nations, in order to contribute to the maintenance of international peace and security, undertake to make available to the Security Council, on its call and in accordance with a special agreement or agreements, armed forces, assistance, and facilities, including rights of passage, necessary for the purpose of maintaining international peace and security.

2. Such agreement or agreements shall govern the numbers and types of forces, their degree of readiness and general location, and the nature of the facilities and assistance to be provided.

3. The agreement or agreements shall be negotiated as soon as possible on the initiative of the Security Council. They shall be concluded between the Security Council and Members or between the Security Council and groups of Members and shall be subject to ratification by the signatory states in accordance with their respective constitutional processes.

Article 44

When the Security Council has decided to use force it shall, before calling upon a Member not represented on it to provide armed forces in fulfillment of the obligations assumed under Article 43, invite that Member, if the Member so desires, to participate in the decisions of the Security Council concerning the employment of contingents of that Member's armed forces.

Article 45

In order to enable the United Nations to take urgent military measures, Members shall hold immediately available national air-force contingents for combined international enforcement action. The strength and degree of readiness of these contingents and plans for their combined action shall be determined, within the limits laid down in the special agreement or agreements referred to in Article 43, by the Security Council with the assistance of the Military Staff Committee.

Article 46

Plans for the application of armed force shall be made by the Security Council with the assistance of the Military Staff Committee.

Article 47

1. There shall be established a Military Staff Committee to advise and assist the Security Council on all questions relating to the Security

Council's military requirements for the maintenance of international peace and security, the employment and command of forces placed at its disposal, the regulation of armaments, and possible disarmament.

2. The Military Staff Committee shall consist of the Chiefs of Staff of the permanent members of the Security Council or their representatives. Any Member of the United Nations not permanently represented on the Committees shall be invited by the Committee to be associated with it when the efficient discharge of the Committee's responsibilities requires the participation of that Member in its work.

3. The Military Staff Committee shall be responsible under the Security Council for the strategic direction of any armed forces placed at the disposal of the Security Council. Questions relating to the command of such forces shall be worked out subsequently.

4. The Military Staff Committee, with the authorization of the Security Council and after consultation with appropriate regional agencies, may establish regional subcommittees.

Article 48

1. The action required to carry out the decisions of the Security Council for the maintenance of international peace and security shall be taken by all the Members of the United Nations or by some of them, as the Security Council may determine.

2. Such decisions shall be carried out by the Members of the United Nations directly and through their action in the appropriate international agencies of which they are members.

Article 49

The Members of the United Nations shall join in affording mutual assistance in carrying out the measures decided upon by the Security Council.

Article 50

If preventive or enforcement measures against any state are taken by the Security Council, any other state, whether a Member of the United Nations or not, which finds itself confronted with special economic problems arising from the carrying out of those measures shall have the right to consult the Security Council with regard to a solution of those problems.

Article 51

Nothing in the present Charter shall impair the inherent right of individual or collective self-defense if an armed attack occurs against a Member of the United Nations, until the Security Council has taken measures necessary to maintain international peace and security. Measures taken by Members in the exercise of this right of self-defense shall be immediately reported to the Security Council and shall not in any way affect the authority and responsibility of the Security Council under the present Charter to take at any time such action as it deems necessary in order to maintain or restore international peace and security.

Chapter VIII

REGIONAL ARRANGEMENTS

Article 52

1. Nothing in the present Charter precludes the existence of regional arrangements or agencies for dealing with such matters relating to the maintenance of international peace and security as are appropriate for regional action, provided that such arrangements or agencies and their activities are consistent with the Purposes and Principles of the United Nations.

2. The Members of the United Nations entering into such arrangements or constituting such agencies shall make every effort to achieve pacific settlement of local disputes through such regional arrangements or by such regional agencies before referring them to the Security Council.

3. The Security Council shall encourage the development of pacific settlement of local disputes through such regional arrangements or by such regional agencies either on the initiative of the states concerned or by reference from the Security Council.

4. This Article in no way impairs the application of Articles 34 and 35.

Article 53

1. The Security Council shall, where appropriate, utilize such regional arrangements or agencies for enforcement action under its authority. But no enforcement action shall be taken under regional arrangements or by regional agencies without the authorization of the Security Council, with the exception of measures against any enemy state, as defined in paragraph 2 of this Article, provided for pursuant to Article 107 or in

regional arrangements directed against renewal of aggressive policy on the part of any such state, until such time as the Organization may, on request of the Governments concerned, be charged with the responsibility for preventing further aggression by such a state.

2. The term enemy state as used in paragraph 1 of this Article applies to any state which during the Second World War has been an enemy of any signatory of the present Charter.

Article 54

The Security Council shall at all times be kept fully informed of activities undertaken or in contemplation under regional arrangements or by regional agencies for the maintenance of international peace and security.

Chapter IX

INTERNATIONAL ECONOMIC AND SOCIAL COOPERATION

Article 55

With a view to the creation of conditions of stability and well-being which are necessary for peaceful and friendly relations among nations based on respect for the principle of equal rights and self-determination of peoples, the United Nations shall promote:

a. higher standards of living, full employment, and conditions of economic and social progress and development;

b. solutions of international economic, social, health, and related problems; and international cultural and educational cooperation; and

c. universal respect for, and observance of, human rights and fundamental freedoms for all without distinction as to race, sex, language, or religion.

Article 56

All Members pledge themselves to take joint and separate action in cooperation with the Organization for the achievement of the purposes set forth in Article 55.

Article 57

1. The various specialized agencies, established by intergovernmental agreement and having wide international responsibilities, as defined in

their basic instruments, in economic, social, cultural, educational, health, and related fields, shall be brought into relationship with the United Nations in accordance with the provisions of Article 63.

2. Such agencies thus brought into relationship with the United Nations are hereinafter referred to as specialized agencies.

Article 58

The Organization shall make recommendations for the coordination of the policies and activities of the specialized agencies.

Article 59

The Organization shall, where appropriate, initiate negotiations among the states concerned for the creation of any new specialized agencies required for the accomplishment of the purposes set forth in Article 55.

Article 60

Responsibility for the discharge of the functions of the Organization set forth in this Chapter shall be vested in the General Assembly and, under the authority of the General Assembly, in the Economic and Social Council, which shall have for this purpose the powers set forth in Chapter X.

Chapter X

THE ECONOMIC AND SOCIAL COUNCIL

Composition

Article 61

1. The Economic and Social Council shall consist of eighteen Members of the United Nations elected by the General Assembly.

2. Subject to the provisions of paragraph 3, six members of the Economic and Social Council shall be elected each year for a term of three years. A retiring member shall be eligible for immediate re-election.

3. At the first election, eighteen members of the Economic and Social Council shall be chosen. The term of office of six members so chosen shall expire at the end of one year, and of six other members at the end of two years, in accordance with arrangements made by the General Assembly.

4. Each member of the Economic and Social Council shall have one representative.

Functions and Powers

Article 62

1. The Economic and Social Council may make or initiate studies and reports with respect to international economic, social, cultural, educational, health, and related matters and may make recommendations with respect to any such matters to the General Assembly, to the Members of the United Nations, and to the specialized agencies concerned.

2. It may make recommendations for the purpose of promoting respect for, and observance of, human rights and fundamental freedoms for all.

3. It may prepare draft conventions for submission to the General Assembly, with respect to matters falling within its competence.

4. It may call, in accordance with the rules prescribed by the United Nations, international conferences on matters falling within its competence.

Article 63

1. The Economic and Social Council may enter into agreements with any of the agencies referred to in Article 57, defining the terms on which the agency concerned shall be brought into relationship with the United Nations. Such agreements shall be subject to approval by the General Assembly.

2. It may coordinate the activities of the specialized agencies through consultation with and recommendations to such agencies and through recommendations to the General Assembly and to the Members of the United Nations.

Article 64

1. The Economic and Social Council may take appropriate steps to obtain regular reports from the specialized agencies. It may make arrangements with the Members of the United Nations and with the specialized agencies to obtain reports on the steps taken to give effect to its own recommendations and to recommendations on matters falling within its competence made by the General Assembly.

2. It may communicate its observations on these reports to the General Assembly.

Article 65

The Economic and Social Council may furnish information to the Security Council and shall assist the Security Council upon its request.

Article 66

1. The Economic and Social Council shall perform such functions as fall within its competence in connection with the carrying out of the recommendations of the General Assembly.

2. It may, with the approval of the General Assembly, perform services at the request of Members of the United Nations and at the request of specialized agencies.

3. It shall perform such other functions as are specified elsewhere in the present Charter or as may be assigned to it by the General Assembly.

Voting

Article 67

1. Each member of the Economic and Social Council shall have one vote.

2. Decisions of the Economic and Social Council shall be made by a majority of the members present and voting.

Procedure

Article 68

The Economic and Social Council shall set up commissions in economic and social fields and for the promotion of human rights, and for such other commissions as may be required for the performance of its functions.

Article 69

The Economic and Social Council shall invite any Member of the United Nations to participate, without vote, in its deliberations on any matter of particular concern to that Member.

Article 70

The Economic and Social Council may make arrangements for representatives of the specialized agencies to participate, without vote, in its deliberations and in those of the commissions established by it, and for its representatives to participate in the deliberations of the specialized agencies.

Article 71

The Economic and Social Council may make suitable arrangements for consultation with non-governmental organizations which are concerned with matters within its competence. Such arrangements may be made with international organizations and, where appropriate, with national organizations after consultation with the Member of the United Nations concerned.

Article 72

1. The Economic and Social Council shall adopt its own rules of procedure, including the method of selecting its President.

2. The Economic and Social Council shall meet as required in accordance with its rules, which shall include provision for the convening of meetings on the request of a majority of its members.

Chapter XI

DECLARATION REGARDING NON-SELF-GOVERNING TERRITORIES

Article 73

Members of the United Nations which have or assume responsibilities for the administration of territories whose peoples have not yet attained a full measure of self-government recognize the principle that the interests of the inhabitants of these territories are paramount, and accept as a sacred trust the obligation to promote to the utmost, within the system of international peace and security established by the present Charter, the well-being of the inhabitants of these territories, and, to this end:

a. to ensure, with due respect for the culture of the peoples concerned, their political, economic, social, and educational advancement, their just treatment, and their protection against abuses;

b. to develop self-government, to take due account of the political aspirations of the peoples, and to assist them in the progressive development of their free political institutions, according to the particular circumstances of each territory and its peoples and their varying stages of advancement;

c. to further international peace and security;

d. to promote constructive measures of development, to encourage research, and to cooperate with one another and, when and where appropriate, with specialized international bodies with a view to the practical achievement of the social, economic, and scientific purposes set forth in this Article; and

e. to transmit regularly to the Secretary-General for information purposes, subject to such limitation as security and constitutional considerations may require, statistical and other information of a technical nature relating to economic, social, and educational conditions in the territories for which they are respectively responsible other than those territories to which Chapters XII and XIII apply.

Article 74

Members of the United Nations also agree that their policy in respect of the territories to which this Chapter applies, no less than in respect of their metropolitan areas, must be based on the general principle of good-neighborliness, due account being taken of the interests and well-being of the rest of the world, in social, economic, and commercial matters.

CHAPTER XII

INTERNATIONAL TRUSTEESHIP SYSTEM

Article 75

The United Nations shall establish under its authority an international trusteeship system for the administration and supervision of such territories as may be placed thereunder by subsequent individual agreements. These territories are hereinafter referred to as trust territories.

Article 76

The basic objectives of the trusteeship system, in accordance with the Purposes of the United Nations laid down in Article 1 of the present Charter, shall be:

a. to further international peace and security;

b. to promote the political, economic, social, and educational advancement of the inhabitants of the trust territories, and their progressive development towards self-government or independence as may be appropriate to the particular circumstances of each territory and its peoples and the freely expressed wishes of the peoples concerned, and as may be provided by the terms of each trusteeship agreement;

c. to encourage respect for human rights and for fundamental freedoms for all without distinction as to race, sex, language, or religion, and to encourage recognition of the interdependence of the peoples of the world; and

d. to ensure equal treatment in social, economic, and commercial matters for all Members of the United Nations and their nationals, and also equal treatment for the latter in the administration of justice, without prejudice to the attainment of the foregoing objectives and subject to the provisions of Article 80.

Article 77

1. The trusteeship system shall apply to such territories in the following categories as may be placed thereunder by means of trusteeship agreements:

a. territories now held under mandate;

b. territories which may be detached from enemy states as a result of the Second World War; and

c. territories voluntarily placed under the system by states responsible for their administration.

2. It will be a matter for subsequent agreement as to which territories in the foregoing categories will be brought under the trusteeship system and upon what terms.

Article 78

The trusteeship system shall not apply to territories which have become Members of the United Nations, relationship among which shall be based on respect for the principle of sovereign equality.

Article 79

The terms of trusteeship for each territory to be placed under the trusteeship system, including any alteration or amendment, shall be agreed upon by the states directly concerned, including the mandatory power in the case of territories held under mandate by a Member of the United Nations, and shall be approved as provided for in Articles 83 and 85.

Article 80

1. Except as may be agreed upon in individual trusteeship agreements, made under Articles 77, 79, and 81, placing each territory under the trusteeship system, and until such agreements have been concluded, nothing in this Chapter shall be construed in or of itself to alter in any manner the rights whatsoever of any states or any peoples or the

terms of existing international instruments to which Members of the United Nations may respectively be parties.

2. Paragraph 1 of this Article shall not be interpreted as giving grounds for delay or postponement of the negotiation and conclusion of agreements for placing mandated and other territories under the trusteeship system as provided for in Article 77.

Article 81

The trusteeship agreement shall in each case include the terms under which the trust territory will be administered and designate the authority which will exercise the administration of the trust territory. Such authority, hereinafter called the administering authority, may be one or more states or the Organization itself.

Article 82

There may be designated, in any trusteeship agreement, a strategic area or areas which may include part or all of the trust territory to which the agreement applies, without prejudice to any special agreement or agreements made under Article 43.

Article 83

1. All functions of the United Nations relating to strategic areas, including the approval of the terms of the trusteeship agreements and of their alteration or amendment, shall be exercised by the Security Council.

2. The basic objectives set forth in Article 76 shall be applicable to the people of each strategic area.

3. The Security Council shall, subject to the provisions of the trusteeship agreements and without prejudice to security considerations, avail itself of the assistance of the Trusteeship Council to perform those functions of the United Nations under the trusteeship system relating to political, economic, social, and educational matters in the strategic areas.

Article 84

It shall be the duty of the administering authority to ensure that the trust territory shall play its part in the maintenance of international peace and security. To this end the administering authority may make use of volunteer forces, facilities, and assistance from the trust territory in carrying out the obligations towards the Security Council undertaken in this regard by the administering authority, as well as for local defense and the maintenance of law and order within the trust territory.

Article 85

1. The functions of the United Nations with regard to trusteeship agreements for all areas not designated as strategic, including the approval of the terms of the trusteeship agreements and of their alteration or amendment, shall be exercised by the General Assembly.

2. The Trusteeship Council, operating under the authority of the General Assembly, shall assist the General Assembly in carrying out these functions.

Chapter XIII

THE TRUSTEESHIP COUNCIL

Composition

Article 86

1. The Trusteeship Council shall consist of the following Members of the United Nations:

a. those Members administering trust territories;

b. such of those Members mentioned by name in Article 23 as are not administering trust territories; and

c. as many other Members elected for three-year terms by the General Assembly as may be necessary to ensure that the total number of members of the Trusteeship Council is equally divided between those Members of the United Nations which administer trust territories and those which do not.

2. Each member of the Trusteeship Council shall designate one specially qualified person to represent it therein.

Functions and Powers

Article 87

The General Assembly and, under its authority, the Trusteeship Council, in carrying out their functions, may:

a. consider reports submitted by the administering authority;

b. accept petitions and examine them in consultation with the administering authority;

c. provide for periodic visits to the respective trust territories at times agreed upon with the administering authority; and

d. take these and other actions in conformity with the terms of the trusteeship agreements.

Article 88

The Trusteeship Council shall formulate a questionnaire on the political, economic, social, and educational advancement of the inhabitants of each trust territory, and the administering authority for each trust territory within the competence of the General Assembly shall make an annual report to the General Assembly upon the basis of such questionnaire.

Voting

Article 89

1. Each member of the Trusteeship Council shall have one vote.

2. Decisions of the Trusteeship Council shall be made by a majority of the members present and voting.

Procedure

Article 90

1. The Trusteeship Council shall adopt its own rules of procedure, including the method of selecting its President.

2. The Trusteeship Council shall meet as required in accordance with its rules, which shall include provision for the convening of meetings on the request of a majority of its members.

Article 91

The Trusteeship Council shall, when appropriate, avail itself of the assistance of the Economic and Social Council and of the specialized agencies in regard to matters with which they are respectively concerned.

Chapter XIV

THE INTERNATIONAL COURT OF JUSTICE

Article 92

The International Court of Justice shall be the principal judicial organ of the United Nations. It shall function in accordance with the annexed Statute, which is based upon the Statute of the Permanent Court of International Justice and forms an integral part of the present Charter.

Article 93

1. All Members of the United Nations are *ipso facto* parties to the Statute of the International Court of Justice.

2. A state which is not a Member of the United Nations may become a party to the Statute of the International Court of Justice on conditions to be determined in each case by the General Assembly upon the recommendation of the Security Council.

Article 94

1. Each Member of the United Nations undertakes to comply with the decision of the International Court of Justice in any case to which it is a party.

2. If any party to a case fails to perform the obligations incumbent upon it under a judgment rendered by the Court, the other party may have recourse to the Security Council, which may, if it deems necessary, make recommendations or decide upon measures to be taken to give effect to the judgment.

Article 95

Nothing in the present Charter shall prevent Members of the United Nations from entrusting the solution of their differences to other tribunals by virtue of agreements already in existence or which may be concluded in the future.

Article 96

1. The General Assembly or the Security Council may request the International Court of Justice to give an advisory opinion on any legal question.

2. Other organs of the United Nations and specialized agencies, which may at any time be so authorized by the General Assembly, may also request advisory opinions of the Court on legal questions arising within the scope of their activities.

Chapter XV

THE SECRETARIAT

Article 97

The Secretariat shall comprise a Secretary-General and such staff as the Organization may require. The Secretary-General shall be appointed by the General Assembly upon the recommendation of the Security Council. He shall be the chief administrative officer of the Organization.

Article 98

The Secretary-General shall act in that capacity in all meetings of the General Assembly, of the Security Council, of the Economic and Social Council, and of the Trusteeship Council, and shall perform such other functions as are entrusted to him by these organs. The Secretary-General shall make an annual report to the General Assembly on the work of the Organization.

Article 99

The Secretary-General may bring to the attention of the Security Council any matter which in his opinion may threaten the maintenance of international peace and security.

Article 100

1. In the performance of their duties the Secretary-General and the staff shall not seek or receive instructions from any government or from any other authority external to the Organization. They shall refrain from any action which might reflect on their position as international officials responsible only to the Organization.

2. Each Member of the United Nations undertakes to respect the exclusively international character of the responsibilities of the Secretary-General and the staff and not to seek to influence them in the discharge of their responsibilities.

Article 101

1. The staff shall be appointed by the Secretary-General under regulations established by the General Assembly.

2. Appropriate staffs shall be permanently assigned to the Economic and Social Council, the Trusteeship Council, and, as required, to other organs of the United Nations. These staffs shall form a part of the Secretariat.

3. The paramount consideration in the employment of the staff and in the determination of the conditions of service shall be the necessity of securing the highest standards of efficiency, competence, and integrity. Due regard shall be paid to the importance of recruiting the staff on as wide a geographical basis as possible.

Chapter XVI

MISCELLANEOUS PROVISIONS

Article 102

1. Every treaty and every international agreement entered into by any Member of the United Nations after the present Charter comes into force shall as soon as possible be registered with the Secretariat and published by it.

2. No party to any such treaty or international agreement which has not been registered in accordance with the provisions of paragraph 1 of this Article may invoke that treaty or agreement before any organ of the United Nations.

Article 103

In the event of a conflict between the obligations of the Members of the United Nations under the present Charter and their obligations under any other international agreement, their obligations under the present Charter shall prevail.

Article 104

The Organization shall enjoy in the territory of each of its Members such legal capacity as may be necessary for the exercise of its functions and the fulfillment of its purposes.

Article 105

1. The Organization shall enjoy in the territory of each of its Members such privileges and immunities as are necessary for the fulfillment of its purposes.

2. Representatives of the Members of the United Nations and officials of the Organization shall similarly enjoy such privileges and immunities as are necessary for the independent exercise of their functions in connection with the Organization.

3. The General Assembly may make recommendations with a view to determining the details of the application of paragraphs 1 and 2 of this Article or may propose conventions to the Members of the United Nations for this purpose.

Chapter XVII

TRANSITIONAL SECURITY ARRANGEMENTS

Article 106

Pending the coming into force of such special agreements referred to in Article 43 as in the opinion of the Security Council enable it to begin the exercise of its responsibilities under Article 42, the parties to the Four-Nation Declaration, signed at Moscow, October 30, 1943, and France, shall, in accordance with the provisions of paragraph 5 of that Declaration, consult with one another and as occasion requires with other Members of the United Nations with a view to such joint action on behalf of the Organization as may be necessary for the purpose of maintaining international peace and security.

Article 107

Nothing in the present Charter shall invalidate or preclude action, in relation to any state which during the Second World War has been an enemy of any signatory to the present Charter, taken or authorized as a result of that war by the Governments having responsibility for such action.

Chapter XVIII

AMENDMENTS

Article 108

Amendments to the present Charter shall come into force for all Members of the United Nations when they have been adopted by a vote of two thirds of the members of the General Assembly and ratified in accordance with their respective constitutional processes by two thirds of the Members of the United Nations, including all the permanent members, of the Security Council.

Article 109

1. A General Conference of the Members of the United Nations for the purpose of reviewing the present Charter may be held at a date and place to be fixed by a two-thirds vote of the members of the General Assembly and by a vote of any seven members of the Security Council. Each Member of the United Nations shall have one vote in the conference.

2. Any alteration of the present Charter recommended by a two-thirds vote of the conference shall take effect when ratified in accordance with their respective constitutional processes by two thirds of the Members of the United Nations including all the permanent members of the Security Council.

3. If such a conference has not been held before the tenth annual session of the General Assembly following the coming into force of the present Charter, the proposal to call such a conference shall be placed on the agenda of that session of the General Assembly, and the conference shall be held if so decided by a majority vote of the members of the General Assembly and by a vote of any seven members of the Security Council.

Chapter XIX

RATIFICATION AND SIGNATURE

Article 110

1. The present Charter shall be ratified by the signatory states in accordance with their respective constitutional processes.

2. The ratifications shall be deposited with the Government of the United States of America, which shall notify all the signatory states of each deposit as well as the Secretary-General of the Organization when he has been appointed.

3. The present Charter shall come into force upon the deposit of ratifications by the Republic of China, France, the Union of Soviet Socialist Republics, the United Kingdom of Great Britain and Northern Ireland, and the United States of America, and by a majority of the other signatory states. A protocol of the ratification deposited shall thereupon be drawn up by the Government of the United States of America which shall communicate copies thereof to all the signatory states.

4. The states signatory to the present Charter which ratify it after it has come into force will become original Members of the United Nations on the date of the deposit of their respective ratifications.

Article 111

The present Charter, of which the Chinese, French, Russian, English, and Spanish texts are equally authentic, shall remain deposited in the archives of the Government of the United States of America. Duly certified copies thereof shall be transmitted by that Government to the Governments of the other signatory states.

IN FAITH WHEREOF the representatives of the Governments of the United Nations have signed the present Charter.

DONE at the city of San Francisco the twenty-sixth day of June, one thousand nine hundred and forty-five.

STATUTE OF THE INTERNATIONAL COURT OF JUSTICE

Article 1

The INTERNATIONAL COURT OF JUSTICE established by the Charter of the United Nations as the principal judicial organ of the United Nations shall be constituted and shall function in accordance with the provisions of the present Statute.

Chapter I

ORGANIZATION OF THE COURT

Article 2

The Court shall be composed of a body of independent judges, elected regardless of their nationality from among persons of high moral character, who possess the qualifications required in their respective countries for appointment to the highest judicial offices, or are jurisconsults of recognized competence in international law.

Article 3

1. The Court shall consist of fifteen members, no two of whom may be nationals of the same state.

2. A person who for the purposes of membership in the Court could be regarded as a national of more than one state shall be deemed to be a national of the one in which he ordinarily exercises civil and political rights.

Article 4

1. The members of the Court shall be elected by the General Assembly and by the Security Council from a list of persons nominated by the national groups in the Permanent Court of Arbitration, in accordance with the following provisions.

2. In the case of Members of the United Nations not represented in the Permanent Court of Arbitration, candidates shall be nominated by national groups appointed for this purpose by their governments under the same conditions as those prescribed for members of the Permanent

Court of Arbitration by Article 44 of the Convention of The Hague of 1907 for the pacific settlement of international disputes.

3. The conditions under which a state which is a party to the present Statute but is not a Member of the United Nations may participate in electing the members of the Court shall, in the absence of a special agreement, be laid down by the General Assembly upon recommendation of the Security Council.

Article 5

1. At least three months before the date of the election, the Secretary-General of the United Nations shall address a written request to the members of the Permanent Court of Arbitration belonging to the states which are parties to the present Statute, and to the members of the national groups appointed under Article 4, paragraph 2, inviting them to undertake, within a given time, by national groups, the nomination of persons in a position to accept the duties of a member of the Court.

2. No group may nominate more than four persons, not more than two of whom shall be of their own nationality. In no case may the number of candidates nominated by a group be more than double the number of seats to be filled.

Article 6

Before making these nominations, each national group is recommended to consult its highest court of justice, its legal faculties and schools of law, and its national academies and national sections of international academies devoted to the study of law.

Article 7

1. The Secretary-General shall prepare a list in alphabetical order of all the persons thus nominated. Save as provided in Article 12, paragraph 2, these shall be the only persons eligible.

2. The Secretary-General shall submit this list to the General Assembly and to the Security Council.

Article 8

The General Assembly and the Security Council shall proceed independently of one another to elect the members of the Court.

Article 9

At every election, the electors shall bear in mind not only that the persons to be elected should individually possess the qualifications required, but also that in the body as a whole the representation of the main forms of civilization and of the principal legal systems of the world should be assured.

Article 10

1. Those candidates who obtain an absolute majority of votes in the General Assembly and in the Security Council shall be considered as elected.

2. Any vote of the Security Council, whether for the election of judges or for the appointment of members of the conference envisaged in Article 12, shall be taken without any distinction between permanent and non-permanent members of the Security Council.

3. In the event of more than one national of the same state obtaining an absolute majority of the votes both of the General Assembly and of the Security Council, the eldest of these only shall be considered as elected.

Article 11

If, after the first meeting held for the purpose of the election, one or more seats remain to be filled, a second and, if necessary, a third meeting shall take place.

Article 12

1. If, after the third meeting, one or more seats still remain unfilled, a joint conference consisting of six members, three appointed by the General Assembly and three by the Security Council, may be formed at any time at the request of either the General Assembly or the Security Council, for the purpose of choosing by the vote of an absolute majority one name for each seat still vacant, to submit to the General Assembly and the Security Council for their respective acceptance.

2. If the joint conference is unanimously agreed upon any person who fulfils the required conditions, he may be included in its list, even though he was not included in the list of nominations referred to in Article 7.

3. If the joint conference is satisfied that it will not be successful in procuring an election, those members of the Court who have already been elected shall, within a period to be fixed by the Security Council, proceed to fill the vacant seats by selection from among those candidates who have obtained votes either in the General Assembly or in the Security Council.

4. In the event of an equality of votes among the judges, the eldest judge shall have a casting vote.

Article 13

1. The members of the Court shall be elected for nine years and may be re-elected; provided, however, that of the judges elected at the first election, the terms of five judges shall expire at the end of three years and the terms of five more judges shall expire at the end of six years.

2. The judges whose terms are to expire at the end of the above-mentioned initial periods of three and six years shall be chosen by lot to be drawn by the Secretary-General immediately after the first election has been completed.

3. The members of the Court shall continue to discharge their duties until their places have been filled. Though replaced, they shall finish any cases which they may have begun.

4. In the case of the resignation of a member of the Court, the resignation shall be addressed to the President of the Court for transmission to the Secretary-General. This last notification makes the place vacant.

Article 14

Vacancies shall be filled by the same method as that laid down for the first election, subject to the following provision: the Secretary-General shall, within one month of the occurrence of the vacancy, proceed to issue the invitations provided for in Article 5, and the date of the election shall be fixed by the Security Council.

Article 15

A member of the Court elected to replace a member whose term of office has not expired shall hold office for the remainder of his predecessor's term.

Article 16

1. No member of the Court may exercise any political or administrative function, or engage in any other occupation of a professional nature.

2. Any doubt on this point shall be settled by the decision of the Court.

Article 17

1. No member of the Court may act as agent, counsel, or advocate in any case.

2. No member may participate in the decision of any case in which he has previously taken part as agent, counsel, or advocate for one of the parties, or as a member of a national or international court, or of a commission of enquiry, or in any other capacity.

3. Any doubt on this point shall be settled by the decision of the Court.

Article 18

1. No member of the Court can be dismissed unless, in the unanimous opinion of the other members, he has ceased to fulfil the required conditions.

2. Formal notification thereof shall be made to the Secretary-General by the Registrar.

3. This notification makes the place vacant.

Article 19

The members of the Court, when engaged on the business of the Court, shall enjoy diplomatic privileges and immunities.

Article 20

Every member of the Court shall, before taking up his duties, make a solemn declaration in open court that he will exercise his powers impartially and conscientiously.

Article 21

1. The Court shall elect its President and Vice-President for three years; they may be re-elected.

2. The Court shall appoint its Registrar and may provide for the appointment of such other officers as may be necessary.

Article 22

1. The seat of the court shall be established at The Hague. This, however, shall not prevent the Court from sitting and exercising its functions elsewhere whenever the Court considers it desirable.

2. The President and the Registrar shall reside at the seat of the Court.

Article 23

1. The Court shall remain permanently in session, except during the judicial vacations, the dates and duration of which shall be fixed by the Court.

2. Members of the Court are entitled to periodic leave, the dates and duration of which shall be fixed by the Court, having in mind the distance between The Hague and the home of each judge.

3. Members of the Court shall be bound, unless they are on leave or prevented from attending by illness or other serious reasons duly explained to the President, to hold themselves permanently at the disposal of the Court.

Article 24

1. If, for some special reason, a member of the Court considers that he should not take part in the decision of a particular case, he shall so inform the President.

2. If the President considers that for some special reason one of the members of the Court should not sit in a particular case, he shall give him notice accordingly.

3. If in any such case the member of the Court and the President disagree, the matter shall be settled by the decision of the Court.

Article 25

1. The full Court shall sit except when it is expressly provided otherwise in the present Statute.

2. Subject to the condition that the number of judges available to constitute the Court is not thereby reduced below eleven, the Rules of the Court may provide for allowing one or more judges, according to circumstances and in rotation, to be dispensed from sitting.

3. A quorum of nine judges shall suffice to constitute the Court.

Article 26

1. The Court may from time to time form one or more chambers, composed of three or more judges as the Court may determine, for dealing with particular categories of cases; for example, labor cases and cases relating to transit and communications.

2. The Court may at any time form a chamber for dealing with a particular case. The number of judges to constitute such a chamber shall be determined by the Court with the approval of the parties.

3. Cases shall be heard and determined by the chambers provided for in this Article if the parties so request.

Article 27

A judgment given by any of the chambers provided for in Articles 26 and 29 shall be considered as rendered by the Court.

Article 28

The chambers provided for in Articles 26 and 29 may, with the consent of the parties, sit and exercise their functions elsewhere than at The Hague.

Article 29

With a view to the speedy despatch of business, the Court shall form annually a chamber composed of five judges which, at the request of the parties, may hear and determine cases by summary procedure. In addition, two judges shall be selected for the purpose of replacing judges who find it impossible to sit.

Article 30

1. The Court shall frame rules for carrying out its functions. In particular, it shall lay down rules of procedure.

2. The Rules of the Court may provide for assessors to sit with the Court or with any of its chambers, without the right to vote.

Article 31

1. Judges of the nationality of each of the parties shall retain their right to sit in the case before the Court.

2. If the Court includes upon the Bench a judge of the nationality of one of the parties, any other party may choose a person to sit as judge. Such person shall be chosen preferably from among those persons who have been nominated as candidates as provided in Articles 4 and 5.

3. If the Court includes upon the Bench no judge of the nationality of the parties, each of these parties may proceed to choose a judge as provided in paragraph 2 of this Article.

4. The provisions of this Article shall apply to the case of Articles 26 and 29. In such cases, the President shall request one or, if necessary, two of the members of the Court forming the chamber to give place to the members of the Court of the nationality of the parties concerned, and, failing such, or if they are unable to be present, to the judges specially chosen by the parties.

5. Should there be several parties in the same interest, they shall, for the purpose of the preceding provisions, be reckoned as one party only. Any doubt upon this point shall be settled by the decision of the Court.

6. Judges chosen as laid down in paragraphs 2, 3, and 4 of this Article shall fulfil the conditions required by Articles 2, 17 (paragraph 2), 20,

and 24 of the present Statute. They shall take part in the decision on terms of complete equality with their colleagues.

Article 32

1. Each member of the Court shall receive an annual salary.

2. The President shall receive a special annual allowance.

3. The Vice-President shall receive a special allowance for every day on which he acts as President.

4. The judges chosen under Article 31, other than members of the Court, shall receive compensation for each day on which they exercise their functions.

5. These salaries, allowances, and compensation shall be fixed by the General Assembly. They may not be decreased during the term of office.

6. The salary of the Registrar shall be fixed by the General Assembly on the proposal of the Court.

7. Regulations made by the General Assembly shall fix the conditions under which retirement pensions may be given to members of the Court and to the Registrar, and the conditions under which members of the Court and the Registrar shall have their traveling expenses refunded.

8. The above salaries, allowances, and compensation shall be free of all taxation.

Article 33

The expenses of the Court shall be borne by the United Nations in such a manner as shall be decided by the General Assembly.

Chapter II

COMPETENCE OF THE COURT

Article 34

1. Only states may be parties in cases before the Court.

2. The Court, subject to and in conformity with its Rules, may request of public international organizations information relevant to cases before it, and shall receive such information presented by such organizations on their own initiative.

3. Whenever the construction of the constituent instrument of a public international organization or of an international convention adopted thereunder is in question in a case before the Court, the Registrar shall

so notify the public international organization concerned and shall communicate to it copies of all the written proceedings.

Article 35

1. The Court shall be open to the states parties to the present Statute.

2. The conditions under which the Court shall be open to other states shall, subject to the special provisions contained in treaties in force, be laid down by the Security Council, but in no case shall such conditions place the parties in a position of inequality before the Court.

3. When a state which is not a Member of the United Nations is a party to a case, the Court shall fix the amount which that party is to contribute towards the expenses of the Court. This provision shall not apply if such state is bearing a share of the expenses of the Court.

Article 36

1. The jurisdiction of the Court comprises all cases which the parties refer to it and all matters specially provided for in the Charter of the United Nations or in treaties and conventions in force.

2. The states parties to the present Statute may at any time declare that they recognize as compulsory *ipso facto* and without special agreement, in relation to any other state accepting the same obligation, the jurisdiction of the Court in all legal disputes concerning:

  a. the interpretation of a treaty;

  b. any question of international law;

  c. the existence of any fact which, if established, would constitute a breach of an international obligation;

  d. the nature or extent of the reparation to be made for the breach of an international obligation.

3. The declarations referred to above may be made unconditionally or on condition of reciprocity on the part of several or certain states, or for a certain time.

4. Such declarations shall be deposited with the Secretary-General of the United Nations, who shall transmit copies thereof to the parties to the Statute and to the Registrar of the Court.

5. Declarations made under Article 36 of the Statute of the Permanent Court of International Justice and which are still in force shall be deemed, as between the parties to the present Statute, to be acceptances

of the compulsory jurisdiction of the International Court of Justice for the period which they still have to run and in accordance with their terms.

6. In the event of a dispute as to whether the Court has jurisdiction, the matter shall be settled by the decision of the Court.

Article 37

Whenever a treaty or convention in force provides for reference of a matter to a tribunal to have been instituted by the League of Nations, or to the Permanent Court of International Justice, the matter shall, as between the parties to the present Statute, be referred to the International Court of Justice.

Article 38

1. The Court, whose function is to decide in accordance with international law such disputes as are submitted to it, shall apply:

a. international conventions, whether general or particular, establishing rules expressly recognized by the contesting states;

b. international custom, as evidence of a general practice accepted as law;

c. the general principles of law recognized by civilized nations;

d. subject to the provisions of Article 59, judicial decisions and the teachings of the most highly qualified publicists of the various nations, as subsidiary means for the determination of rules of law.

2. This provision shall not prejudice the power of the Court to decide a case *ex aequo et bono,* if the parties agree thereto.

Chapter III

PROCEDURE

Article 39

1. The official languages of the Court shall be French and English. If the parties agree that the case shall be conducted in French, the judgment shall be delivered in French. If the parties agree that the case shall be conducted in English, the judgment shall be delivered in English.

2. In the absence of an agreement as to which language shall be employed, each party may, in the pleadings, use the language which it prefers; the decision of the Court shall be given in French and English. In this case the Court shall at the same time determine which of the two texts shall be considered as authoritative.

3. The Court shall, at the request of any party, authorize a language other than French or English to be used by that party.

Article 40

1. Cases are brought before the Court, as the case may be, either by the notification of the special agreement or by a written application addressed to the Registrar. In either case the subject of the dispute and the parties shall be indicated.

2. The Registrar shall forthwith communicate the application to all concerned.

3. He shall also notify the Members of the United Nations through the Secretary-General, and also any other states entitled to appear before the Court.

Article 41

1. The Court shall have the power to indicate, if it considers that circumstances so require, any provisional measures which ought to be taken to preserve the respective rights of either party.

2. Pending the final decision, notice of the measures suggested shall forthwith be given to the parties and to the Security Council.

Article 42

1. The parties shall be represented by agents.

2. They may have the assistance of counsel or advocates before the Court.

3. The agents, counsel, and advocates of parties before the Court shall enjoy the privileges and immunities necessary to the independent exercise of their duties.

Article 43

1. The procedure shall consist of two parts: written and oral.

2. The written proceedings shall consist of the communication to the Court and to the parties of memorials, counter-memorials and, if necessary, replies; also all papers and documents in support.

3. These communications shall be made through the Registrar, in the order and within the time fixed by the Court.

4. A certified copy of every document produced by one party shall be communicated to the other party.

5. The oral proceedings shall consist of the hearing by the Court of witnesses, experts, agents, counsel, and advocates.

Article 44

1. For the service of all notices upon persons other than the agents, counsel, and advocates, the Court shall apply direct to the government of the state upon whose territory the notice has to be served.

2. The same provision shall apply whenever steps are to be taken to procure evidence on the spot.

Article 45

The hearing shall be under the control of the President or, if he is unable to preside, of the Vice-President; if neither is able to preside, the senior judge present shall preside.

Article 46

The hearing in Court shall be public, unless the Court shall decide otherwise, or unless the parties demand that the public be not admitted.

Article 47

1. Minutes shall be made at each hearing and signed by the Registrar and the President.

2. These minutes alone shall be authentic.

Article 48

The Court shall make orders for the conduct of the case, shall decide the form and time in which each party must conclude its arguments, and make all arrangements connected with the taking of evidence.

Article 49

The Court may, even before the hearing begins, call upon the agents to produce any document or to supply any explanations. Formal note shall be taken of any refusal.

Article 50

The Court may, at any time, entrust any individual, body, bureau, commission, or other organization that it may select, with the task of carrying out an enquiry or giving an expert opinion.

Article 51

During the hearing any relevant questions are to be put to the witnesses and experts under the conditions laid down by the Court in the rules of procedure referred to in Article 30.

Article 52

After the Court has received the proofs and evidence within the time specified for the purpose, it may refuse to accept any further oral or written evidence that one party may desire to present unless the other side consents.

Article 53

1. Whenever one of the parties does not appear before the Court, or fails to defend its case, the other party may call upon the Court to decide in favor of its claim.

2. The Court must, before doing so, satisfy itself, not only that it has jurisdiction in accordance with Articles 36 and 37, but also that the claim is well founded in fact and law.

Article 54

1. When, subject to the control of the Court, the agents, counsel, and advocates have completed their presentation of the case, the President shall declare the hearing closed.

2. The Court shall withdraw to consider the judgment.

3. The deliberations of the Court shall take place in private and remain secret.

Article 55

1. All questions shall be decided by a majority of the judges present.

2. In the event of an equality of votes, the President or the judge who acts in his place shall have a casting vote.

Article 56

1. The judgment shall state the reasons on which it is based.

2. It shall contain the names of the judges who have taken part in the decision.

Article 57

If the judgment does not represent in whole or in part the unanimous opinion of the judges, any judge shall be entitled to deliver a separate opinion.

Article 58

The judgment shall be signed by the President and by the Registrar. It shall be read in open court, due notice having been given to the agents.

Article 59

The decision of the Court has no binding force except between the parties and in respect of that particular case.

Article 60

The judgment is final and without appeal. In the event of dispute as to the meaning or scope of the judgment, the Court shall construe it upon the request of any party.

Article 61

1. An application for revision of a judgment may be made only when it is based upon the discovery of some fact of such a nature as to be a decisive factor, which fact was, when the judgment was given, unknown to the Court and also to the party claiming revision, always provided that such ignorance was not due to negligence.

2. The proceedings for revision shall be opened by a judgment of the Court expressly recording the existence of the new fact, recognizing that it has such a character as to lay the case open to revision, and declaring the application admissible on this ground.

3. The Court may require previous compliance with the terms of the judgment before it admits proceedings in revision.

4. The application for revision must be made at latest within six months of the discovery of the new fact.

5. No application for revision may be made after the lapse of ten years from the date of the judgment.

Article 62

1. Should a state consider that it has an interest of a legal nature which may be affected by the decision in the case, it may submit a request to the Court to be permitted to intervene.

2. It shall be for the Court to decide upon this request.

Article 63

1. Whenever the construction of a convention to which states other than those concerned in the case are parties is in question, the Registrar shall notify all such states forthwith.

2. Every state so notified has the right to intervene in the proceedings; but if it uses this right, the construction given by the judgment will be equally binding upon it.

Article 64

Unless otherwise decided by the Court, each party shall bear its own costs.

Chapter IV

ADVISORY OPINIONS

Article 65

1. The Court may give an advisory opinion on any legal question at the request of whatever body may be authorized by or in accordance with the Charter of the United Nations to make such a request.

2. Questions upon which the advisory opinion of the Court is asked shall be laid before the Court by means of a written request containing an exact statement of the question upon which an opinion is required, and accompanied by all documents likely to throw light upon the question.

Article 66

1. The Registrar shall forthwith give notice of the request for an advisory opinion to all states entitled to appear before the Court.

2. The Registrar shall also, by means of a special and direct communication, notify any state entitled to appear before the Court or international organization considered by the Court, or, should it not be sitting, by the President, as likely to be able to furnish information on the question, that the Court will be prepared to receive, within a time limit to be fixed by the President, written statements, or to hear, at a public sitting to be held for the purpose, oral statements relating to the question.

3. Should any such state entitled to appear before the Court have failed to receive the special communication referred to in paragraph 2 of this Article, such state may express a desire to submit a written statement or to be heard; and the Court will decide.

4. States and organizations having presented written or oral statements or both shall be permitted to comment on the statements made by other states or organizations in the form, to the extent, and within the time limits which the Court, or, should it not be sitting, the President, shall decide in each particular case. Accordingly, the Registrar shall in due time communicate any such written statements to states and organizations having submitted similar statements.

Article 67

The Court shall deliver its advisory opinions in open court, notice having been given to the Secretary-General and to the representatives of Members of the United Nations, of other states and of international organizations immediately concerned.

Article 68

In the exercise of its advisory functions the Court shall further be guided by the provisions of the present Statute which apply in contentious cases to the extent to which it recognizes them to be applicable.

Chapter V

AMENDMENT

Article 69

Amendments to the present Statute shall be effected by the same procedure as is provided by the Charter of the United Nations for amendments to that Charter, subject however to any provisions which the General Assembly upon recommendations of the Security Council may adopt concerning the participation of states which are parties to the present Statute but are not Members of the United Nations.

Article 70

The Court shall have power to propose such amendments to the present Statute as it may deem necessary, through written communications to the Secretary-General, for consideration in conformity with the provisions of Article 69.

Universal Declaration of Human Rights

Adopted by the United Nations
General Assembly, December 10, 1948

PREAMBLE

WHEREAS recognition of the inherent dignity and of the equal and inalienable rights of all members of the human family is the foundation of freedom, justice and peace in the world,

WHEREAS disregard and contempt for human rights have resulted in barbarous acts which have outraged the conscience of mankind, and the advent of a world in which human beings shall enjoy freedom of speech and belief and freedom from fear and want has been proclaimed as the highest aspiration of the common people,

WHEREAS it is essential, if man is not to be compelled to have recourse, as a last resort, to rebellion against tyranny and oppression, that human rights should be protected by the rule of law,

WHEREAS it is essential to promote the development of friendly relations between nations,

WHEREAS the peoples of the United Nations have in the Charter reaffirmed their faith in fundamental human rights, in the dignity and worth of the human person and in the equal rights of men and women and have determined to promote social progress and better standards of life in larger freedom,

WHEREAS Member States have pledged themselves to achieve, in co-operation with the United Nations, the promotion of universal respect for and observance of human rights and fundamental freedoms,

WHEREAS a common understanding of these rights and freedoms is of the greatest importance for the full realization of this pledge,

NOW, THEREFORE,

The General Assembly

Proclaims this Universal Declaration of Human Rights as a common standard of achievement for all peoples and all nations, to the end that every individual and every organ of society, keeping this Declaration constantly in mind, shall strive by teaching and education to promote respect for these rights and freedoms and by progressive measures, national and international, to secure their universal and effective recognition and observance, both among the peoples of Member States themselves and among the peoples of territories under their jurisdiction.

ARTICLE 1.

All human beings are born free and equal in dignity and rights. They are endowed with reason and conscience and should act towards one another in a spirit of brotherhood.

ARTICLE 2.

Everyone is entitled to all the rights and freedoms set forth in this Declaration without distinction of any kind, such as race, color, sex, language, religion, political or other opinion, national or social origin, property, birth or other status.

Furthermore, no distinction shall be made on the basis of the political, jurisdictional or international status of the county or territory to which a person belongs, whether it be independent, trust, non-self-governing or under any other limitation of sovereignty.

ARTICLE 3.

Everyone has the right to life, liberty and security of person.

ARTICLE 4.

No one shall be held in slavery or servitude; slavery and the slave trade shall be prohibited in all their forms.

ARTICLE 5.

No one shall be subjected to torture or to cruel, inhuman or degrading treatment or punishment.

ARTICLE 6.

Everyone has the right to recognition everywhere as a person before the law.

ARTICLE 7.

All are equal before the law and are entitled without any discrimination to equal protection of the law. All are entitled to equal protection against any discrimination in violation of this Declaration and against any incitement to such discrimination.

ARTICLE 8.

Everyone has the right to an effective remedy by the competent national tribunals for acts violating the fundamental rights granted him by the constitution or by law.

ARTICLE 9.

No one shall be subjected to arbitrary arrest, detention, or exile.

ARTICLE 10.

Everyone is entitled in full equality to a fair and public hearing by an independent and impartial tribunal, in the determination of his rights and obligations and of any criminal charge against him.

ARTICLE 11.

1. Everyone charged with a penal offense has the right to be presumed innocent until proved guilty according to law in a public trial at which he has had all the guarantees necessary for his defense.

2. No one shall be held guilty of any penal offense on account of any act or omission which did not constitute a penal offense, under national or international law, at the time when it was committed. Nor shall a heavier penalty be imposed than the one that was applicable at the time the penal offense was committed.

ARTICLE 12.

No one shall be subjected to arbitrary interference with his privacy, family, home or correspondence nor to attacks upon his honor and reputation.

Everyone has the right to the protection of the law against such interference or attacks.

ARTICLE 13.

1. Everyone has the right to freedom of movement and residence within the borders of each state.

2. Everyone has the right to leave any country, including his own, and to return to his country.

ARTICLE 14.

1. Everyone has the right to seek and to enjoy in other countries asylum from persecution.

2. This right may not be invoked in the case of prosecutions genuinely arising from non-political crimes or from acts contrary to the purposes and principles of the United Nations.

ARTICLE 15.

1. Everyone has the right to a nationality.

2. No one shall be arbitrarily deprived of his nationality nor denied the right to change his nationality.

ARTICLE 16.

1. Men and women of full age, without any limitation due to race, nationality or religion, have the right to marry and to found a family. They are entitled to equal rights as to marriage, during marriage and at its dissolution.

2. Marriage shall be entered into only with the free and full consent of the intending spouses.

3. The family is the natural and fundamental group unit of society and is entitled to protection by society and the state.

ARTICLE 17.

1. Everyone has the right to own property alone as well as in association with others.

2. No one shall be arbitrarily deprived of his property.

ARTICLE 18.

Everyone has the right to freedom of thought, conscience and religion; this right includes freedom to change his religion or belief, and freedom, either alone or in community with others and in public or private, to manifest his religion or belief in teaching, practice, worship and observance.

ARTICLE 19.

Everyone has the right to freedom of opinion and expression; this right includes freedom to hold opinions without interference and to seek, receive and impart information and ideas through any media and regardless of frontiers.

ARTICLE 20.

1. Everyone has the right to freedom of peaceful assembly and association.

2. No one may be compelled to belong to an association.

ARTICLE 21.

1. Everyone has the right to take part in the government of his country, directly or through freely chosen representatives.

2. Everyone has the right of equal access to public service in his country.

3. The will of the people shall be the basis of the authority of government; this will shall be expressed in periodic and genuine elections which shall be by universal and equal suffrage and shall be held by secret vote or by equivalent free voting procedures.

ARTICLE 22.

Everyone, as a member of society, has the right to social security and is entitled to realization, through national effort and international cooperation and in accordance with the organization and resources of each state, of the economic, social and cultural rights indispensable for his dignity and the free development of his personality.

ARTICLE 23.

1. Everyone has the right to work, to free choice of employment, to just and favorable conditions of work and to protection against unemployment.

2. Everyone, without any discrimination, has the right to equal pay for equal work.

3. Everyone who works has the right to just and favorable remuneration ensuring for himself and his family an existence worthy of human dignity, and supplemented, if necessary, by other means of social protection.

4. Everyone has the right to form and to join trade unions for the protection of his interests.

ARTICLE 24.

Everyone has the right to rest and leisure, including reasonable limitation of working hours and periodic holidays with pay.

ARTICLE 25.

1. Everyone has the right to a standard of living adequate for the health and well-being of himself and of his family, including food, clothing, housing and medical care and necessary social services, and the right to security in the event of unemployment, sickness, disability, widowhood, old age or other lack of livelihood in circumstances beyond his control.

2. Motherhood and childhood are entitled to special care and assistance. All children, whether born in or out of wedlock, shall enjoy the same social protection.

ARTICLE 26.

1. Everyone has the right to education. Education shall be free, at least in the elementary and fundamental stages. Elementary education shall be compulsory. Technical and professional education shall be made generally available and higher education shall be equally accessible to all on the basis of merit.

2. Education shall be directed to the full development of the human personality and to the strengthening of respect for human rights and fundamental freedoms. It shall promote understanding, tolerance and friendship among all nations, racial or religious groups, and shall further the activities of the United Nations for the maintenance of peace.

3. Parents have a prior right to choose the kind of education that shall be given to their children.

ARTICLE 27.

1. Everyone has the right freely to participate in the cultural life of the community, to enjoy the arts and to share in scientific advancement and its benefits.

2. Everyone has the right to the protection of the moral and material interests resulting from any scientific, literary, or artistic production of which he is the author.

ARTICLE 28.

Everyone is entitled to a social and international order in which the rights and freedoms set forth in this Declaration can be fully realized.

ARTICLE 29.

1. Everyone has duties to the community, in which alone the free and full development of his personality is possible.

2. In the exercise of his rights and freedoms, everyone shall be subject only to such limitations as are determined by law solely for the purpose of securing due recognition and respect for the rights and freedoms of others and of meeting the just requirements of morality, public order and the general welfare in a democratic society.

3. These rights and freedoms may in no case be exercised contrary to the purposes and principles of the United Nations.

ARTICLE 30.

Nothing in this Declaration may be interpreted as implying for any state, group or person any right to engage in any activity or to perform any act aimed at the destruction of any of the rights and freedoms set forth herein.

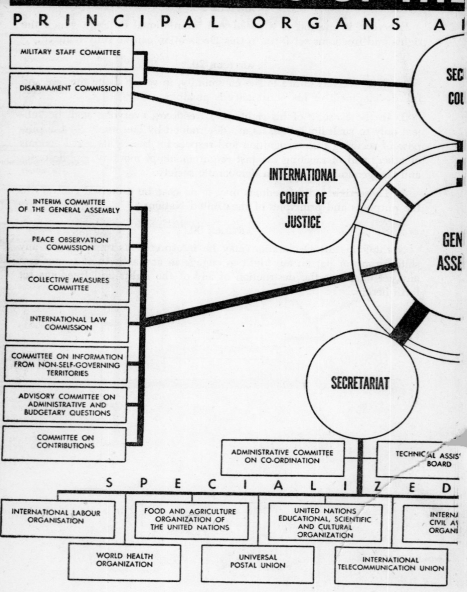

MILITARY STAFF COMMITTEE

DISARMAMENT COMMISSION

SEC
COL

INTERNATIONAL
COURT OF
JUSTICE

GEN
ASSE

INTERIM COMMITTEE
OF THE GENERAL ASSEMBLY

PEACE OBSERVATION
COMMISSION

COLLECTIVE MEASURES
COMMITTEE

INTERNATIONAL LAW
COMMISSION

COMMITTEE ON INFORMATION
FROM NON-SELF-GOVERNING
TERRITORIES

ADVISORY COMMITTEE ON
ADMINISTRATIVE AND
BUDGETARY QUESTIONS

COMMITTEE ON
CONTRIBUTIONS

SECRETARIAT

ADMINISTRATIVE COMMITTEE
ON CO-ORDINATION

TECHNICAL ASSIST
BOARD

S P E C I A L I Z E D

INTERNATIONAL LABOUR
ORGANISATION

FOOD AND AGRICULTURE
ORGANIZATION OF
THE UNITED NATIONS

UNITED NATIONS
EDUCATIONAL, SCIENTIFIC
AND CULTURAL
ORGANIZATION

INTERNA
CIVIL A
ORGANI

WORLD HEALTH
ORGANIZATION

UNIVERSAL
POSTAL UNION

INTERNATIONAL
TELECOMMUNICATION UNION

UNITED NATIONS

ND SUBSIDIARY BODIES

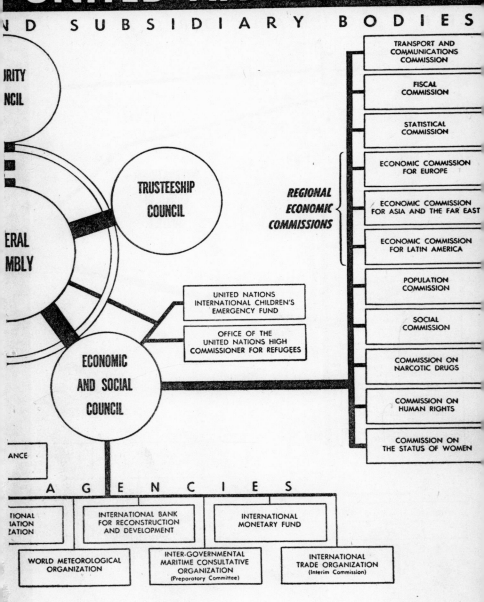

TRANSPORT AND
COMMUNICATIONS
COMMISSION

FISCAL
COMMISSION

STATISTICAL
COMMISSION

ECONOMIC COMMISSION
FOR EUROPE

ECONOMIC COMMISSION
FOR ASIA AND THE FAR EAST

ECONOMIC COMMISSION
FOR LATIN AMERICA

*REGIONAL
ECONOMIC
COMMISSIONS*

POPULATION
COMMISSION

SOCIAL
COMMISSION

COMMISSION ON
NARCOTIC DRUGS

COMMISSION ON
HUMAN RIGHTS

COMMISSION ON
THE STATUS OF WOMEN

URITY
NCIL

TRUSTEESHIP
COUNCIL

ERAL
MBLY

UNITED NATIONS
INTERNATIONAL CHILDREN'S
EMERGENCY FUND

OFFICE OF THE
UNITED NATIONS HIGH
COMMISSIONER FOR REFUGEES

ECONOMIC
AND SOCIAL
COUNCIL

ANCE

A G E N C I E S

TIONAL
IATION
ZATION

INTERNATIONAL BANK
FOR RECONSTRUCTION
AND DEVELOPMENT

INTERNATIONAL
MONETARY FUND

WORLD METEOROLOGICAL
ORGANIZATION

INTER-GOVERNMENTAL
MARITIME CONSULTATIVE
ORGANIZATION
(Preparatory Committee)

INTERNATIONAL
TRADE ORGANIZATION
(Interim Commission)

Members of the UN

(Dates indicate entry into the UN of non-charter members.)

Afghanistan (Nov. 19, 1946)
Argentina
Australia
Belgium
Bolivia
Brazil
Burma (Apr. 19, 1948)
Byelorussian Soviet Socialist Republic
Canada
Chile
China
Colombia
Costa Rica
Cuba
Czechoslovakia
Denmark
Dominican Republic
Ecuador
Egypt
El Salvador
Ethiopia
France
Greece
Guatemala
Haiti
Honduras
Iceland (Nov. 19, 1946)
India
Indonesia (Sept. 28, 1950)
Iran
Iraq
Israel (May 11, 1949)
Lebanon
Liberia
Luxembourg
Mexico
Netherlands
New Zealand
Nicaragua
Norway
Pakistan (Sept. 30, 1947)
Panama
Paraguay
Peru
Philippines
Poland
Saudi Arabia
Sweden (Nov. 19, 1946)
Syria
Thailand (Dec. 16, 1946)
Turkey
Ukrainian Soviet Socialist Republic
Union of South Africa
Union of Soviet Socialist Republics
United Kingdom of Great Britain and Northern Ireland
United States of America
Uruguay
Venezuela
Yugoslavia

Abbreviations

UN, United Nations
Bank, International Bank for Reconstruction and Development
ECAFE, Economic Commission for Asia and the Far East
ECE, Economic Commission for Europe
ECLA, Economic Commission for Latin America
ECOSOC, Economic and Social Council
FAO, Food and Agriculture Organization
Fund, International Monetary Fund
GA, General Assembly
GATT, General Agreement on Tariffs and Trade
ICAO, International Civil Aviation Organization
ICJ, International Court of Justice
ILC, International Law Commission
ILO, International Labour Organisation
IMCO, Inter-Governmental Maritime Consultative Organization
IPPC, International Penal and Penitentiary Commission
ITO, International Trade Organization
ITS, International Tracing Service
ITU, International Telecommunication Union
NGO's, Non-Governmental Organizations
NSG, Non-self-governing Territories
SC, Security Council
SG, Secretary-General
TAA, Technical Assistance Administration
TAB, Technical Assistance Board
UNESCO, United Nations Educational, Scientific and Cultural Organization
UNICEF, United Nations International Children's Fund
UNKRA, United Nations Korean Reconstruction Agency
UNRWA, United Nations Relief and Works Agency
UPU, Universal Postal Union
WHO, World Health Organization
WMO, World Meteorological Organization

Index

231

2236-6